SUCCESS FOR SCHOOLS

SCIENCE

3

TEACHING RESOURCES

PHOTOCOPIABLE

Janet Harper • Steve Hearn • Ann Tiernan

Published by Letts Educational
The Chiswick Centre
414 Chiswick High Road
London W4 5TF

020 89963333
020 87428390
mail@lettsed.co.uk
www.letts-education.com

Letts Educational is part of the Granada Learning Group. Granada Learning is a division of Granada plc.

Text: © Janet Harper, Steve Hearn, Ann Tiernan 2004

First published 2004

ISBN 184315191X

Acknowledgements

Commissioned by Helen Clark

Project management by Vicky Butt

Editing by Pat Winter

With thanks to Anne Saunders

Illustrations by Phillip Burrows and Graham-Cameron Illustration (Ann Biggs)

Photographs on pp 94, 96, 103, 104 from Steve Hearn

Cover design by Ken Vail Graphic Design, Cambridge

Internal design by Ken Vail Graphic Design, Cambridge

Production by PDQ

Printed and bound by Ashford Colour Press

Internet safety notice

Whilst Letts has made all reasonable enquiries to ensure all the third party websites listed in this publication are suitable for KS3 students, Letts Educational does not endorse or approve the content of any such third party websites nor does it accept responsibility or liability for their content. Further, Letts makes no warranty or representation about anything contained in such third party websites referred to herein nor that their URLs will continue to be maintained, available and accessible and accepts no liability in connection with any suggestion or claim that any such third party website breaches any law or regulation or in any other way infringes on any of your rights. Also, you acknowledge that internet sites can change very quickly and Letts Educational accepts no responsibility or liability for any subsequent changes to the contents of any such third party websites, their URLs and/or any other online material.

Letts Educational strongly advises teachers, parents and/or guardians to access, review and monitor all such third party websites before directing students to them and also generally for schools actively to encourage parental supervision of students who are accessing the internet at home.

For government guidance on internet safety in schools, please see:

safety.ngfl.gov.uk/schools

For government advice on internet safety for parents, please see:

safety.ngfl.gov.uk/parents

Contents

Curriculum and contents matching grid

Biology: life processes and living things

Lesson heading	Teacher page	Student page	Framework objectives	SoW	NC
Unit 1					
Inheriting genes	1	20	C3	9A	Sc2:1d,4a
Collecting environmental data that affects variation	2	22	SE4, SE5, SE6	9A	Sc1:2e,2g–l Sc2:4a
Selective breeding	3	24	C3	9A	Sc2:4c
Investigating selective breeding	4	26	SE4, SE5, SE6	9A	Sc1:2a,2d, 2e,2g–k
Cloning	5	28	C3, SE1	9A	Sc1:1a Sc2:1d,4c
Unit 2					
A fit body	6	30	C2, SE5	9B	Sc1:2g,2i Sc2: 2n
Breathing for oxygen	7	32	C1, C2	9B	Sc2:2i–l
The effects of smoking and drugs	8	34	C2, SE1	9B	Sc1:1a,2i Sc2:2i,2m
Finding a balance	9	36	C2, SE1–SE3	9B	Sc1:1a–c Sc2:2a,2e
Unit 3					
What is photosynthesis?	10	38	C4, C5, I1	9C	Sc2:3a,3b
Leaves: the organs of photosynthesis	11	40	C4	9C	Sc2:1b,1c,1e
The rate of photosynthesis	12	42	C4, SE3, SE6, SE7	9C	Sc1:2j,2k, 2m–o Sc2:3a
Maximising plant growth	13	44	C4, SE6	9C	Sc1:2j,2k,2m Sc2:3c,3d
The products of photosynthesis	14	46	C1, C4, C5	9C	Sc1:2c Sc2:3a,3b,3e
The importance of photosynthesis	15	48	I1–I3, C4, C5	9C	Sc2:5a,5b,5e
Unit 4					
Food production by plants	16	50	I1	9D	Sc1:2j,2k Sc2:5e
The effect of fertilisers on plant growth	17	52	C4, SE2, SE7	9D	Sc1:2d,2e Sc2:3c
Competition	18	54	I1, I2, SE2, SE4	9D	Sc1:2d,2e Sc2:5d,5e
Balancing the environment	19	56	I1–I3	9D	Sc2:5a,5f

Objectives are numbered consecutively as laid out in the *Framework for Teaching Science*.
C = Cells, I = Interdependence, P = Particles, E = Energy, F = Forces, SE = Scientific Enquiry

Chemistry: materials and their properties

	Lesson heading	Teacher page	Student page	Framework objectives	SoW	NC
Unit 5	Properties of metals	20	58	SE1, SE5	9E	Sc1:2j,2k,2m, Sc3:1a,1c,1d
	Acids and metals	21	60	P2–P4	9E	Sc1:2f,2k,2m, Sc3:1c,1f,2h,3a,3e,3h
	Carbonates and oxides	22	62	P2, P3, SE4, SE5, SE7	9E	Sc1: 2f,2k,2m, Sc3:1c,1f,2g,2h,3a,3e,3g,3h
	Neutralisation	23	64	P1–P3	9E	Sc1:2f,2g, Sc3:1c,1f,2g,2h,3d,3f,3h
Unit 6	Metal reactions	24	66	P4, P5, SE6, SE7	9F	Sc1:1b,2a,2d,2f,2m,2o, Sc3:1c,1f,2g,2h,3a,3c,3d,3h
	Acid reactions	25	68	P1, P3, P5, SE2–SE6	9F	Sc1:2a,2c–k,2m, Sc3:1c,1f,2g,2h,3a,3c,3e,3h
	Displacement	26	70	P1–P5, SE6	9F	Sc1:2c,2f,2i,2k,2m, Sc3:1c,1f,2g,2h,3b,3c,3h
	Extracting metals	27	72	P4, P5, SE1	9F	Sc1:2j,2k,2m, Sc3:1c,2f,2h,3h
Unit 7	Soils	28	74	SE1	9G	Sc1:2f,2i,2m, Sc3:2h,3d,3f
	Acid rain	29	76	P3, SE1, SE4, SE5	9G	Sc1:2f,2g,2i–k, Sc3:1c,2i,3e,3g
	Solving the acid rain problem	30	78	P1, P3	9G	Sc1:2f,2k,2m, Sc3:1c,2i,3e–g
	Climate change	31	80	SE1, SE6, SE7	9G	Sc1:1a,1c,2o, Sc3:2i
Unit 8	Energy from fuels	32	82	SE2, SE4, SE5	9H	Sc1:1c,2a,2e–h,2j,2k,2m, Sc3:1c,1f,2h,2i
	Energy from chemical reactions	33	84	P1, P5, SE4–SE6	9H	Sc1:2f,2g,2i–k,2m, Sc3:2h,3b,3c,3h
	The chemical industry	34	86	P1, SE1, SE5	9H	Sc1:1a,1c, 2f,2k,2m, Sc3:2h
	Mass and chemical change	35	88	P1–P3 SE5	9H	Sc1:2f,2g,2l,2m, Sc3:1c,1f,2g,3h

Objectives are numbered consecutively as laid out in the *Framework for Teaching Science*.
C = Cells, I = Interdependence, P = Particles, E = Energy, F = Forces, SE = Scientific Enquiry

Physics: physical processes

Objectives are numbered consecutively as laid out in the *Framework for Teaching Science*.
C = Cells, I = Interdependence, P = Particles, E = Energy, F = Forces, SE = Scientific Enquiry

Introduction

This book is the third in a series that provides a complete Key Stage 3 course in Science. Any school that follows this course will fulfil the teaching requirements as laid down in:

- the QCA Scheme of Work
- the Framework for Teaching Science
- the National Curriculum.

Curriculum matching

The Framework and the National Curriculum

The *Framework for Teaching Science* provides a teaching strategy and is linked to the Scheme of Work and the National Curriculum.

The Framework gives clear yearly teaching objectives which define what students need to know at the end of Year 7, Year 8 and Year 9. The objectives are divided into 5 key ideas:

- cells
- interdependence
- particles
- energy
- forces.

These concepts are developed throughout *Success for Schools Science*. They are clearly introduced in Year 7, and in Years 8 and 9 the work continues to be divided into these groupings. Each Student Book contains dedicated Introduction to Key Ideas pages (pp10–19).

The curriculum and contents matching grid on pages iv to vi of these Teaching Resources links each lesson of the Student Book to the yearly teaching objectives. In the grid:

- C = cells
- I = interdependence
- P = particles
- E = energy
- F = forces.

However, in Years 7 and 8, the yearly teaching objectives do not relate to the entire National Curriculum KS3 programme of study – see *Success for Schools Science* Teaching Resources 1 and 2 (page vii). There are units on all programme of study sections in *Success for Schools Science*, and opportunities are also provided for students to develop their skills in line with the Framework objectives for scientific enquiry, denoted SE.

Prior learning

The opening section of the Student Book (pp4–9) reviews the work done by students in Year 8, helping them to relate it to the Year 9 work that lies ahead.

Curriculum matching to support planning

The Contents at the front of the Student Book (pp2–3) provides detailed links between each lesson and the relevant Framework objective(s).

More detailed curriculum information is provided in these Teaching Resources. The grid on pages iv–vi matches the Year 9 content against the Framework, QCA Scheme of Work and National Curriculum. This information is repeated in the teacher's notes for each lesson (pages 1–55 of this book) under the heading 'Curriculum link'. The 'Curriculum link' section also matches the course against the Year 7 and/or Year 8 Scheme of Work to provide teachers with a review of prior learning, and highlights any issues to emphasise or prior misconceptions that may need to be addressed.

Teaching techniques

To make any subject interesting and enjoyable, teachers want to use a variety of techniques. *Success for Schools Science* helps to make this easy by suggesting activities of a greatly varying nature. Care has been taken to make the course inclusive for students of all learning styles. The design of the Student Books themselves aids visual learners, with vibrant colour coding and a non-consecutive yet clearly routed order of content. In addition to a wide range of learning techniques (quizzes, role plays, practical experiments, research, use of ICT, etc) students are also challenged to work in different groupings – on their own, in pairs, in groups or as a class – to achieve a given outcome.

Resources and safety

In addition to notes for teaching staff, these Teaching Resources also contain resource notes for technicians. The lists of resources given for practical activities are stated per group of students.

All schools are strongly advised to check their own school and LEA guidelines on all materials, chemicals and equipment used in this course. Appropriate CLEAPPS Hazcards should be displayed in the classroom.

How to use the Student Book

The **Aims** section lists the major learning points for the lesson ahead in student-friendly language. These are related to the Framework objectives listed in the Contents (pp 2–3).

Each lesson opens with a **Starter activity**. These can take a number of forms, but above all they are interactive and motivating, and anticipate a major idea of the lesson.

The **Links to Other Key Ideas** feature reminds students of prior learning or alerts them to the links across Biology, Chemistry and Physics topics.

The **main lesson ideas** are covered via a series of headed fact panels.

Glossary terms are highlighted and underlined

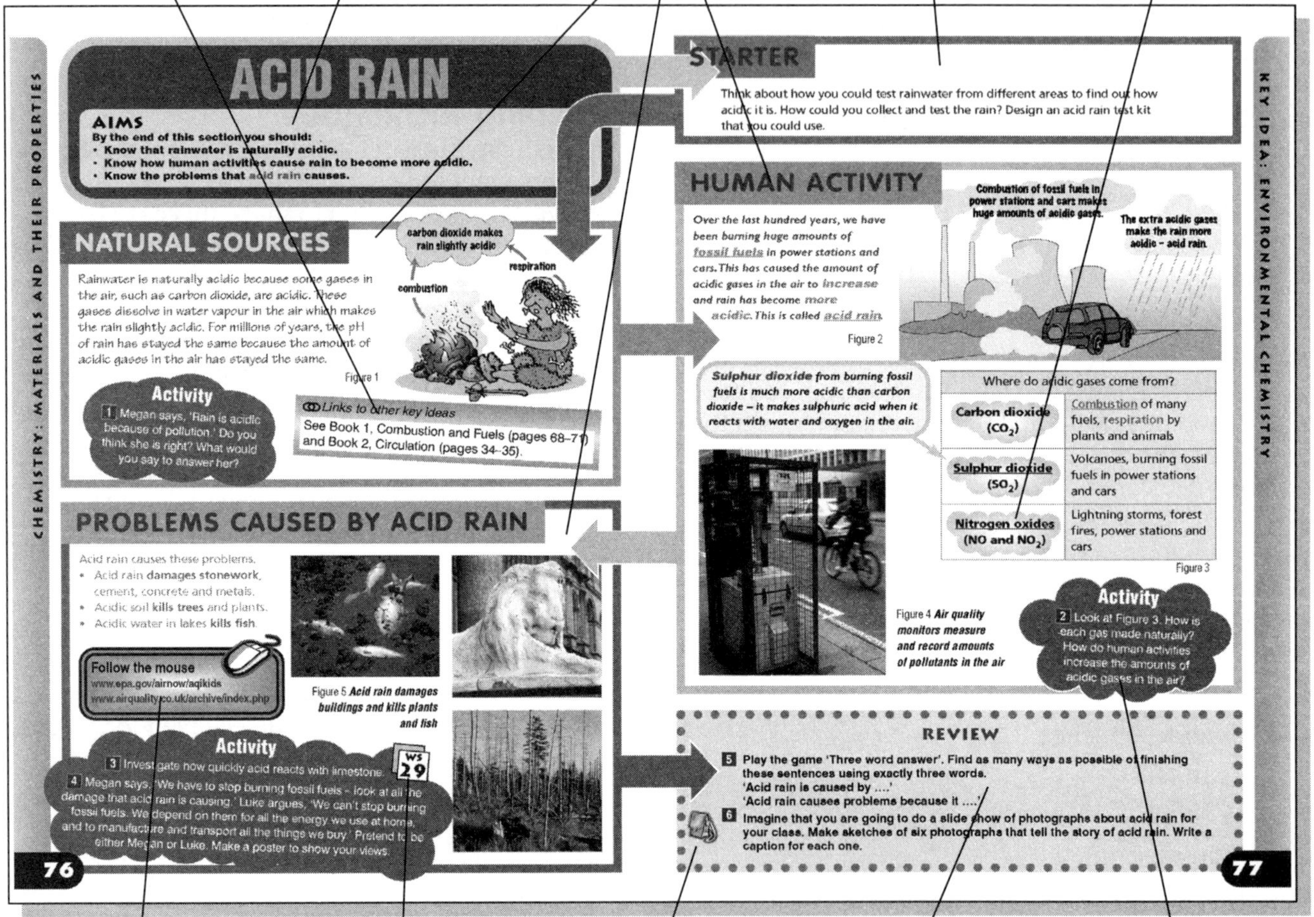

ACID RAIN

AIMS
By the end of this section you should:
* Know that rainwater is naturally acidic.
* Know how human activities cause rain to become more acidic.
* Know the problems that acid rain causes.

NATURAL SOURCES

Rainwater is naturally acidic because some gases in the air, such as carbon dioxide, are acidic. These gases dissolve in water vapour in the air which makes the rain slightly acidic. For millions of years, the pH of rain has stayed the same because the amount of acidic gases in the air has stayed the same.

carbon dioxide makes rain slightly acidic

combustion   respiration

Figure 1

Activity
1 Megan says, 'Rain is acidic because of pollution.' Do you think she is right? What would you say to answer her?

Links to other key ideas
See Book 1, Combustion and Fuels (pages 68–71) and Book 2, Circulation (pages 34–35).

PROBLEMS CAUSED BY ACID RAIN

Acid rain causes these problems.
* Acid rain **damages** stonework, cement, concrete and metals.
* Acidic soil **kills trees** and plants.
* Acidic water in lakes **kills fish**.

Follow the mouse
www.epa.gov/airnow/aqikids
www.airquality.co.uk/archive/index.php

Figure 5 *Acid rain damages buildings and kills plants and fish*

Activity
3 Investigate how quickly acid reacts with limestone.
4 Megan says, 'We have to stop burning fossil fuels – look at all the damage that acid rain is causing.' Luke argues, 'We can't stop burning fossil fuels. We depend on them for all the energy we use at home, and to manufacture and transport all the things we buy.' Pretend to be either Megan or Luke. Make a poster to show your views.

WS 29

76

STARTER

Think about how you could test rainwater from different areas to find out how acidic it is. How could you collect and test the rain? Design an acid rain test kit that you could use.

HUMAN ACTIVITY

Over the last hundred years, we have been burning huge amounts of *fossil fuels* in power stations and cars. This has caused the amount of acidic gases in the air to *increase* and rain has become *more acidic*. This is called *acid rain*.

Combustion of fossil fuels in power stations and cars makes huge amounts of acidic gases. The extra acidic gases make the rain more acidic – acid rain.

Figure 2

Sulphur dioxide from burning fossil fuels is much more acidic than carbon dioxide – it makes sulphuric acid when it reacts with water and oxygen in the air.

Where do acidic gases come from?	
Carbon dioxide (CO$_2$)	Combustion of many fuels, respiration by plants and animals
Sulphur dioxide (SO$_2$)	Volcanoes, burning fossil fuels in power stations and cars
Nitrogen oxides (NO and NO$_2$)	Lightning storms, forest fires, power stations and cars

Figure 3

Figure 4 *Air quality monitors measure and record amounts of pollutants in the air*

Activity
2 Look at Figure 3. How is each gas made naturally? How do human activities increase the amounts of acidic gases in the air?

REVIEW

5 Play the game 'Three word answer'. Find as many ways as possible of finishing these sentences using exactly three words.
'Acid rain is caused by ....'
'Acid rain causes problems because it ....'
6 Imagine that you are going to do a slide show of photographs about acid rain for your class. Make sketches of six photographs that tell the story of acid rain. Write a caption for each one.

77

The **Follow the Mouse** box lists carefully selected web addresses where relevant.

Worksheets are provided to support some activities.

Suitable **homework** questions are indicated by a satchel icon.

Reviews are the plenary sections recommended by the Framework.

Related **activities** aid consolidation and deliver the practical elements of the course.

Arrows direct the student around the spread.

The design of *Success for Schools Science* is highly visual. Many students and teachers will be familiar with this style, popularised by Letts' *Success Guides* revision publications. The colourful and non-consecutive yet clearly routed layout helps to make material accessible and memorable in the classroom.

Student Book structure

The structure of the Student Book is designed to consolidate and support the National Strategy for Teaching Science as laid down in the KS3 Framework document. The Student Book is divided into the following sections:

- **Review** pages for each of Sc2, Sc3 and Sc4 (pp4–9). For Year 7, these pages review work covered at Key Stage 2, for Years 8 and 9 they review work covered earlier in Key Stage 3

- **Introduction to Key Ideas** (pp10–19). These pages introduce the coming year's work

- **Units of work** based on the 13 main topic areas. Each pair of pages is designed to take up one science lesson as detailed on the previous page of this book

- **Revision strategies** (pp130–131). These contain advice for students on organising revision, note making and learning strategies.

- **Assessment** (pp132–137). The end of year test includes questions across the Year 9 units, graded progressively from Level 4 to Level 7.

- **Useful formulae and tables** (pp138–140)

- An integrated **index and glossary** (pp141–143). This section provides definitions of key scientific terms introduced during the current year.

Lesson structure

The *Success for Schools* course delivers the lesson structure recommended by the *Framework for Teaching Science*.

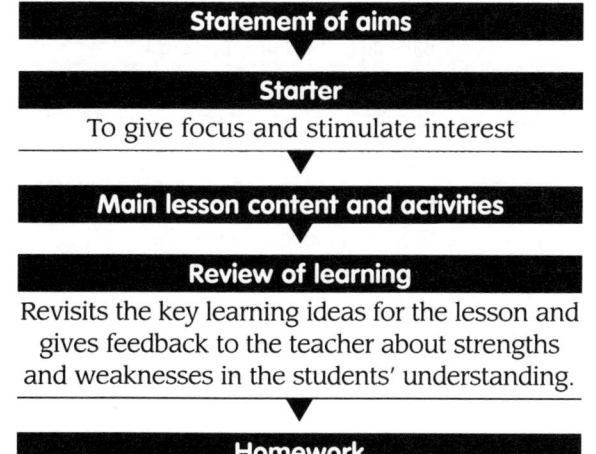

Statement of aims

Starter
To give focus and stimulate interest

Main lesson content and activities

Review of learning
Revisits the key learning ideas for the lesson and gives feedback to the teacher about strengths and weaknesses in the students' understanding.

Homework

Assessment

Success for Schools Science can be used to support your teacher assessment of students throughout Key Stage 3. The course provides:

- A cross-matched grid showing which National Curriculum statements are addressed in each lesson (see ppiv–vi and the individual lesson guidance on pages 1–55 of these Teaching Resources).

- A grid to match each unit of work against Letts *KS3 Success Questions and Answers Levels 3–6* and Letts *KS3 Success Questions and Answers Levels 5–7* (see page x).

- Assessment pages at the end of each Student Book (pp132–137 in Student Book 3) with levelled answers provided on pages xiii and xiv of these Teaching Resources.

- Support for learning and assessment of Sc1 via activities throughout the Student Book and the Investigation support sheets on pages xv and xvi of these Teaching Resources.

Suggested strategies for assessing students:

- Recording **Sc1** level information by monitoring performance against National Curriculum level descriptors using the practical activities in *Success for Schools Science*.

- Using the Investigation support sheets from each *Success for Schools* Teaching Resources Book (ppxv–xvi). These allow students to monitor their own progress through the levels when planning an investigation (Book 1), collecting and analysing data (Book 2) and completing evaluations (Book 3). Comparisons between the sheets and student's own marked work can provide feedback on how to improve next time.

- Using the Assessment pages at the back of the Student Book for **Sc2**, **3** and **4**. The Letts *Questions and Answers* books (see next page) can be used to give additional information about broad level bands.

- Matching students' work to the National Curriculum level descriptors throughout the course.

The National Curriculum level descriptors can be found at **www.nc.uk.net**. Follow the links to view the National Curriculum for KS3 and then choose 'attainment targets' from the menu.

Letts Q & A books

In order to help you assess students' progress and provide your SMT with regular data in the form of National Curriculum levels for each student, *Success for Schools Science* is matched to Letts *KS3 Success Questions and Answers* (both Levels 3–6 and 5–7). These books contain a ready-to-use assessment for each unit in *Success for Schools Science* as shown in the chart below, and come with answer booklets to facilitate marking. A homework diary and progress plotter are included in each book to assist with record keeping and trend tracking.

To order copies of Letts *KS3 Success Questions and Answers* for your school, contact Letts customer services on 0845 6029137.

KS3 Success Questions and Answers Science Levels 3–6 (ISBN 1840859458)

KS3 Success Questions and Answers Science Levels 5–7 (ISBN 1843151383)

Matching *Success for Schools Science* with Letts Q&A books

Student Book 3 units	KS3 Success Q&A Science (Levels 3–6)	KS3 Success Q&A Science (Levels 5–7)
Unit 1 Inheritance and selection	Variation and selective breeding, pp38–39	Variation and selective breeding, pp36–37 Genetics, pp38–39
Unit 2 Fit and healthy	Heart of the matter, pp14–15 Blood & the circulatory system, pp16–17 Skeleton, muscles & joints, pp18–19 The lungs & breathing, pp20–21 Drugs, solvents, alcohol & tobacco, pp26–27 Fighting disease, pp28–29	Heart of the matter, pp14–15 Blood & the circulatory system, pp16–17 Skeleton, muscles & joints, pp18–19 The lungs & breathing, pp20–21 Drugs, solvents, alcohol & tobacco, pp24–25 Fighting disease, pp26–27
Unit 3 Plants and photosynthesis	Photosynthesis, pp30–31	Photosynthesis, pp28–29
Unit 4 Plants for food	Carbon & nitrogen cycles, pp34–35 Food chains & webs, pp40–41	Carbon & nitrogen cycles, pp32–33 Food chains & webs, pp40–41
Unit 5 Reactions of metals and metal compounds	Atoms & elements, pp56–57 Metals, pp58–59 Reactivity series, pp64–65 Acids & alkalis, pp68–69 Making salts, pp70–71 Naming compounds, pp80–81	Atoms & elements, pp56–57 Metals, pp58–59 Reactivity series, pp64–65 Acids & alkalis, pp68–69 Making salts, pp70–71 Naming compounds, pp80–81
Unit 6 Patterns of reactivity	Unusual metals & non-metals, pp60–61 Simple chemical reactions, pp62–63 Reactivity series, pp64–65 Metal displacement reactions, pp66–67	Unusual metals & non-metals, pp60–61 Simple chemical reactions, pp62–63 Reactivity series, pp64–65 Metal displacement reactions, pp66–67
Unit 7 Environmental chemistry	Acids & alkalis, pp68–69	Acids & alkalis, pp68–69
Unit 8 Using chemistry	Compounds, pp78–79 Balancing equations, pp82–83	Compounds, pp78–79 Balancing equations, pp82–83
Unit 9 Energy and electricity	Energy, pp106–107 Circuits, currents and voltage, pp116–117	Energy, pp104–105 Circuits, currents and voltage, pp114–115
Unit 10 Gravity and space	The Earth in space, pp120–121	The Earth in space, pp118–119
Unit 11 Speeding up	Speed, pp84–85 Graphs of motion, pp86–89	Speed, pp84–85 Graphs of motion, pp86–87
Unit 12 Pressure and moments	Moments, pp94–95 Pressure, pp96–97	Moments, pp92–93 Pressure, pp94–95
Unit 13 Investigating scientific questions	–	–

How to use these Teaching Resources

An **ICT opportunity**, such as collecting and processing data using sensors and accessing secondary sources of information via the internet. CD-ROMs and videos can also be useful secondary sources for topics such as genetics and disease, metal extraction from minerals, and animations such as show the effects of gravity and the action of a trebuchet.

WS 8 A cross-reference to the relevant **photocopiable worksheet**(s).

pp 34-35 A cross-reference to the relevant **Student Book** pages.

The **Curriculum link** matches each lesson against the Framework, the QCA Scheme of Work for KS3, and the National Curriculum. Also highlights any issues to consider or potential student misconceptions.

The **Lesson guidance** provides further information on preparing for each lesson; on the resources required; on conducting the practical activities; on likely outcomes.

A **numeracy opportunity**, such as measuring, proportion, drawing bar charts, drawing line graphs.

A **literacy opportunity**, such as extended writing and extracting relevant information. Students will meet technical terms such as *photosynthesis* and *chloroplast* in a scientific context, and should be encouraged to spell the words correctly and to use the Student Book glossary to check their scientific meanings.

The **differentiation** section contains:

● suggestions for adapting the work to improve the performance of low attainers.

● suggestions for extension work for high attainers.

The **technician notes** list resources required for the practical elements of each lesson.

The **safety advice** alerts staff to any potential hazards.

Unit 2 – Fit and healthy

The effects of smoking and drugs **pp 34-35** **WS 8**

UNIT 2 – FIT AND HEALTHY

Curriculum link
NC PoS: Sc2:2i,2m; Sc1:1a,2i
Framework: C2, SE1
QCA SoW: 9B Fit and Healthy
Prior learning: 7A Cells, 7B Reproduction, 8A Food and Digestion, 8B Respiration, 8C Microbes and Disease

Be sensitive to any students who may have had problems or diseases in their family due to drug abuse.

Lesson guidance
Starter suggestions
■ Check that students understand the definition of a drug in the Starter, then read this list: coffee, paracetamol, cough syrup, glue, nail polish remover, hairspray, heroin, aspirin, tobacco, Coca-Cola, opium, LSD, cannabis, amphetamine, tranquilliser, cocaine, alcohol.

Development
■ *Activity 1* should be carried out in a fume cupboard or a well ventilated room, with asthmatics near an open window or door. Demonstrate the amount of tar from burning one cigarette and explain how it stains people's fingers and teeth as well as damaging the lungs. If you are using a fume cupboard, compare a filter cigarette with a non-filter one.

■ *Activity 2* Answers:
(a)

(b) Possible reasons: increased knowledge and education about the effects of smoking on people's health; increased cost (of cigarettes and health/medical/life insurance); increase in the number of public areas where smoking is banned.
(c) Suggestions should include promoting ideas of improved health and saving money.

■ *Activity 3*. Carefully select websites suitable for your students. Each small group researches its allocated drug. Read out the homework and ask groups to collect information for preparing the homework leaflet. Groups can present the Activity 3 information using PowerPoint or a poster. Copy the mind map of Figure 5 onto the board and add the information the groups have found.

Plenary and homework suggestions
■ *Review 4, Worksheet 8* Answers: Caffeine D, Nicotine C, Alcohol H, Amphetamine G, Cocaine A, LSD E, Cannabis B, Heroin F.
■ *Homework 5*. Ask students to use what they have learnt to produce an informative and persuasive leaflet.
Encourage the use of ICT in the production of an interesting design.

Differentiation/extension
■ *Starter*. Explain to more able students that the definition of a drug is actually quite difficult, as even substances like water and vitamins have effects on the functioning of the body.
■ *Activity 3*. Support lower ability students by providing them with a list of websites and particular questions to find the answers to.

Technician notes
Starter
■ whiteboards and pens

Activity 1. Smoking demonstration
Assemble the apparatus shown below:
■ U-tube containing cotton wool or mineral wool
■ rubber bungs and rubber tubing attachments
■ valve attachment to water tap
■ cigarettes, with and without filter

Activity 2. Bar chart
■ graph paper

Activity 3. Drug research
■ access to internet and/or school library

⚠ Safety

Activity 1. should be carried out in a fume cupboard if possible, or in a well ventilated room. Position asthmatics near an open window or door.

8

These Teaching Resources are divided into two sections: lesson guidance for teaching staff and photocopiable resources for use in the classroom.

Teacher's notes

Pages 1–55 of these Teaching Resources contain lesson notes that guide you through the structure of the Student Book (see page viii).

Worksheets

Pages 56–108 of this book contain photocopiable worksheets linked to activities from the Student Book.

Assessment answers

Pages viii–xiv of this book provide the levelled answers to the end of year test given on pages 132–137 of the Student Book.

Investigation support sheets

The factual content and activities in *Success for Schools Science* provide opportunities to teach and assess the Framework objectives for Scientific Enquiry, both as individual skills and as whole investigations.

In addition to the guidance provided in the teacher's notes section, each book of Teaching Resources contains two Investigation Support sheets (pp xv–xvi). Together these form a guide to conducting an investigation which can be referred to throughout the course, whenever students are required to plan, predict, carry out and evaluate a fair test or similar experiment.

In Book 1, these support sheets focused on the steps involved in planning an investigation. In Book 2 they supported the development of data collection and analysis, and in Book 3 they focus on drawing conclusions and evaluating the strength of the evidence. The full set can be used to support students when they are planning, carrying out and writing a report on a full investigation.

Answers to end of year test

1 Using simple physical ideas to explain phenomena is Level 4 in the PoS.

The particles continuously bombard the piston, giving many tiny kicks to it. An average force is generated to balance the load. *(2 marks)*

2 Using scientific names for some major organs of the body systems is Level 4 in the PoS.

a) lungs
b) heart
c) trachea
d) diaphragm *(4 marks)*

3 Identifying the organs of a plant is Level 4 in the PoS.

a) leaf
b) flower
c) stem
d) roots *(2 marks)*

4 Describing the main functions of the organs of a plant is Level 5 in the PoS.

Leaf = Site of photosynthesis where glucose is produced
Flower = Reproductive organ
Stem = Holds the plant upright
Roots = Anchor the plant into the ground and absorb water and minerals from the soil.
(4 marks)

5 Being able to explain the effects of balanced and unbalanced forces is Level 5 in the PoS.

For both Block A and Block B: Resultant vertical force is zero. Resultant horizontal force is 1 N to the right. The blocks accelerate towards the right. *(4 marks)*

(Total *5 marks* if $F = ma$ is used, and acceleration right = 0.5 m/s^2)

6 Being able to use abstract ideas in descriptions of familiar phenomena is Level 5 in the PoS.

a) The car is not accelerating. *(1 mark)*
b) It speed and mass are constant (ignore fuel consumption). *(1 mark)*
c) The thermal energy is being transformed to kinetic energy that moves the car. For energy conservation we argue that the thermal energy accounts for all the original chemical energy, and that the kinetic energy accounts for all the thermal energy. *(2 marks)*

7 Describing the main functions of the organs of the human body is Level 5 in the PoS.

b) and **c)** together, then **a)**, then **d)**. *(3 marks)*

8 Reactions of metals with oxygen and acids is at Level 6 in the PoS. Writing word equations is at Level 6, but, as this questions asks for students to add words to a partially completed equation, this limits the task to Level 5.

a) sodium, calcium, iron, copper *(2 marks)*
(One metal in wrong place: *1 mark*)

b) sodium *(1 mark)*
c) (i) hydrogen *(1 mark)*
(ii) Use a lighted splint *(1 mark)*; when lit, it goes pop *(1 mark)* *(= 2 marks)*
d) Energy is given out; new products are made; not easily reversed; atoms rearranged into new compounds (any two). *(2 marks)*
e) (i) Gains oxygen from the air *(1 mark)*
(ii) oxygen *(1 mark)*; iron oxide *(1 mark)*
(= 2 marks)

9 Reactions of acids to make salts is at Level 6 in the PoS. Separation of mixtures is at Level 5.

a) (i) carbon dioxide *(1 mark)*
(ii) copper chloride *(1 mark)*
(iii) copper sulphate *(1 mark)*
b) Filter *(1 mark)*; evaporate *(1 mark)*; leave some liquid to crystallise slowly *(1 mark)*.
(= 3 marks)

10 Being able to give explanations of phenomena in which a number of factors are considered is Level 6 in the PoS.

a) Mass is the amount of 'stuff' or particles in the material. Weight is force of gravitational attraction between masses. *(1 mark)*
b) The Moon has mass, so there will be a force of gravitational attraction between a person and the Moon, hence the person will have weight. *(1 mark)*

11 Using appropriate scientific terminology when describing life processes is Level 6 in the PoS.

photosynthesis *(1 mark)*

12 Describing some of the causes of variation between living things is Level 6 in the PoS.

Any 3 environmental factors: light levels, availability of water or minerals, space in the soil for root growth, disease etc. *(3 marks)*

13 Describing some of the causes of variation between living things is Level 6 in the PoS.

c) is the correct statement *(1 mark)*

14 Using knowledge of cell structure to explain how cells are adapted to their functions is Level 7 in the PoS.

Root hairs are long and thin to increase surface area for the absorption of water and minerals from the soil and to anchor the plant more firmly in the ground. *(3 marks)*

15 Being able to perform calculations using the correct units is Level 7 in the PoS.

a) Average speed = 100 m/10.03 s = 9.97 m/s (to 3 sig. fig.) *(1 mark)*
b) His speed is changing/increasing from 0 m/s at the start. *(1 mark)*
c) He is running some of the race at a low speed/at less than average speed. *(4 marks)*

16 Being able to explain the motion of bodies in the Solar System using gravity is Level 7 in the PoS.

a)

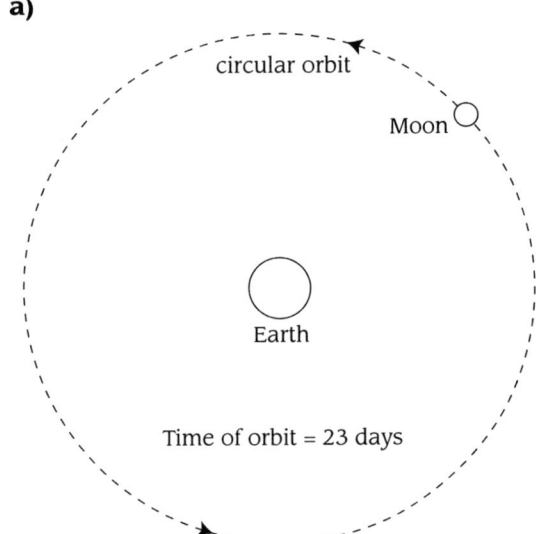

circular orbit

Moon

Earth

Time of orbit = 23 days

(2 marks)

b) The Moon is attracted to the Earth because of gravity. The Moon is moving 'forwards' as well as accelerating towards the Earth, so it falls around the Earth, never getting closer. *(2 marks)*

c) It has the same orbit time as the Earth, and therefore remains stationary over a particular spot on its surface. So a satellite dish can remain stationary and 'see' the satellite without complex tracking equipment *(2 marks)*

17 The recognition of an element in terms of its constituent particles is at Level 7 in the PoS. Recognising symbols and formulae is at Level 7. Discussing acid rain in terms of its reaction with limestone is at Level 7.

a) nitrogen *(1 mark)*

b) any two of: carbon dioxide, sulphur dioxide, water vapour, carbon monoxide *(2 marks)*

c) Environmental problem receives a mark only if linked to the correct pollutant. Any two of: Carbon monoxide *(1 mark)* is toxic/prevents blood from carrying oxygen *(1 mark)*. Carbon dioxide *(1 mark)* (may) cause global warming/an explained outcome of global warming, e.g. sea level rise *(1 mark)*. Sulphur dioxide *(1 mark)* causes acid rain/breathing difficulties/explained outcome of acid rain, e.g. reaction with limestone *(1 mark)*. *(= 4 marks)*

18 Explaining the process of photosynthesis in terms of a chemical change is at Level 7 in the PoS.

a) carbon dioxide and water *(1 mark)*

b) glucose and oxygen *(1 mark)*

c) sunlight energy absorbed by chlorophyll *(1 mark)* *(= 3 marks)*

19 Constructing models to show feeding relationships and explaining how these relationships affect population size is Level 7 in the PoS.

Line 1 is the prey. Line 2 represents the predators. The numbers of predators cannot increase until there has been an increase in the prey population. Similarly, the numbers of predators will decrease after there has been a decrease in the size of the prey population. The line for the predator population, therefore, lags behind the line for the prey population. *(2 marks)*

20 Being able to perform calculations using the correct units is Level 7 in the PoS.

a) 'Balanced' means a situation when all the forces and the moments of the forces cancel each other out. *(2 marks)*

b) X m × 4 N = 0.2 m × 2 N, so X = 0.1 m *(2 marks)*

c) Force R is an upward force balancing the downward forces, so R = 6 N. *(2 marks)*

d) The weight of the beam would act at its centre, 0.15 m from either end. This weight exerts an additional downward force to the right of the pivot, increasing moments on the right and making the beam turn clockwise. So the pivot would have to move right towards the centre of the beam, to equalise moments either side of the pivot and rebalance the beam.

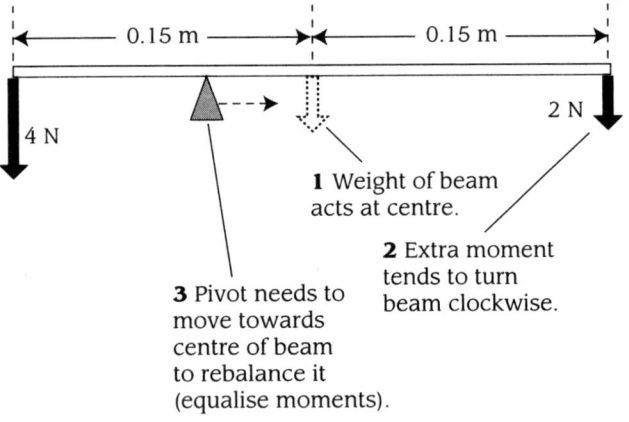

0.15 m ——— 0.15 m

4 N

2 N

1 Weight of beam acts at centre.

2 Extra moment tends to turn beam clockwise.

3 Pivot needs to move towards centre of beam to rebalance it (equalise moments).

(3 marks)

CONCLUDING AND EVALUATING AN INVESTIGATION 1

DRAW CONCLUSIONS

What have you found out?

- What was the relationship you were investigating?
- From the analysis of your data, describe the relationship you have found between the independent and the dependent variable.
- Say whether your prediction was right or wrong.
- Explain, using your scientific knowledge, what happened in the investigation, and why it happened.

ANOMALOUS RESULTS

Did you have any results that did not fit the pattern?

- Look at your graph and label any results that seem odd or out of place compared to the others.
- Explain why you think these happened – your observations during the experiment may help.
- Look at the results from the repeat experiments. Was each repeat exactly the same? If not, how much variation was there?

EVALUATE THE METHOD

- Did the apparatus allow you to measure accurately enough?
- Did you manage to keep the other variables constant for a fair test?
- Explain how you could improve the method you used in the experiment.

SUFFICIENT EVIDENCE

- Did you get enough results to make a firm conclusion?
- Are the results reliable enough to support the conclusion?
- Could you do this investigation in another way to help you explain the relationship between the independent and dependent variables in more detail?

CONCLUDING AND EVALUATING AN INVESTIGATION 2

DRAW CONCLUSIONS

- If you can explain what you have seen and the patterns in the results, then you are working at Level **3**.
- To move to Level **4**, you need to use scientific terms in your conclusion to describe the relationship.
- To work at Level **5** and above, you need to draw conclusions from your results and explain them scientifically – the more detailed and correct your knowledge and understanding, the higher the level.

ANOMALOUS RESULTS

- If you can describe the data you have collected using scientific terms and give the correct units, then you are working at Level **5**.
- To move to Level **6**, you need to identify the results that do not fit the main pattern.

EVALUATE THE METHOD

- If you can suggest improvements, you are working at Level **3**.
- To work at Level **4**, you must give reasons for these improvements.
- If your suggestions are practical, then this is Level **5**.
- To move to Level **6**, explain how these practical suggestions will give you more accurate, sufficient or reliable data.

SUFFICIENT EVIDENCE

- If you are beginning to consider whether the data is sufficient to draw a conclusion, you are working at Level **7**.

Unit 1 - Inheritance and selection

Inheriting genes

pp 20–21 WS 1

Curriculum link

NC PoS: Sc2:1d,4a
Framework: C3
QCA SoW: 9A Inheritance and Selection
Prior learning: 7A Cells, 7B Reproduction, 7D Variation and Classification

Students should know that individuals have characteristics controlled by genes or the environment, and remember that in sexual reproduction the nuclei from male and female sex cells join together.

Throughout this unit, refer to your school's sex education policy and make reference to the PSHCE programme. Be aware of the need for sensitivity towards the personal circumstances of students and their families.

Lesson guidance

Starter suggestions

■ *Worksheet 1.* Draw the attention of students to the fact that the siblings are similar but not identical. Answers:

	Inherited from Dad	Inherited from Mum
Danny	fair curly hair, fingers, legs	shape of eyebrows, eyes, ears, nose, mouth, neck, shoulders
Isabel	eyes, ears, mouth, neck, shoulders, legs	shape of eyebrows, dark straight hair, nose, fingers

Development

■ *Activity 1* Answers:
Male sex cell – nucleus contains chromosomes from the father, tail for movement, head can break through the wall of the ovum; female sex cell – nucleus contains chromosomes from the mother, yolky cytoplasm as a store of energy. Internal fertilisation is when the sperm fertilises the ovum inside the female's body, and external fertilisation is when it happens outside the body. The fertilised ovum uses the yolky cytoplasm for energy so that it can divide into a ball of cells as it travels along the oviduct. The ball of cells, known as an embryo, implants in the wall of the uterus and the placenta develops to pass food and oxygen to it from the mother's blood.

■ *Activity 2.* Place the 46 numbered blue beads in a blue bag to represent the chromosomes in the nucleus of a cell from the father. Place the 46 numbered pink beads in a pink bag to represent the chromosomes in the nucleus of a cell from the mother. Ask a student to pick out 23 beads from each bag to go into each of the sex cells. Notice which numbers are picked so that, when the activity is repeated, the variation can be seen.

■ *Activity 3* Answer: Diagrams should show one sperm cell fertilising one ovum, which then splits into two, with each cell developing into a baby. For example:

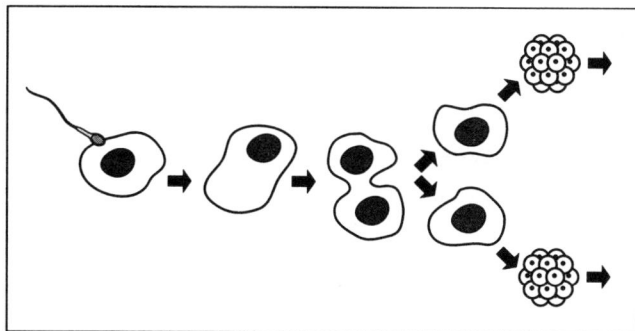

Plenary and homework suggestions

■ *Review 4* is a literacy opportunity.
■ *Homework 5.* Identify the work covered in Year 7 that students particularly need to remind themselves of.

Differentiation/extension

■ *Worksheet 1* and *Activity 2.* Help more able students to make the connection between the fact that siblings will have some characteristics in common because they are inheriting genes from the same parents, and that they are not identical due to the random combination of chromosomes into the sex cells.

Technician notes
Activity 2. Picking beads (class demonstration)
■ 46 blue beads/counters numbered 1–46
■ 46 pink beads/counters numbered 1–46
■ blue bag
■ pink bag

Unit 1 - Inheritance and selection

Collecting environmental data that affects variation

pp 22–23

Curriculum link

NC PoS: Sc2:4a; Sc1:2e,2g–l
Framework: SE4–SE6
QCA SoW: 9A Inheritance and Selection
Prior learning: 7D Variation and Classification

Students should know that individuals of a species show characteristics that may be environmentally determined or inherited.

Lesson guidance

Starter suggestions

■ Students identify the environmental factor that has produced the variation. Answers:
Light. The plant with the elongated stem has been in the dark and has been growing in search of the light.
Weightlifting. The muscles have developed over time due to body-building.
Country born in and language spoken by parents.
Types of food eaten. Rickets is a nutrient deficiency disease.

Development

■ *Activity 1 Answers:* Variation lists for tomatoes may include – size, shape, colour, taste.
■ *Activity 2 Answers:* Characteristics identified in the brainstorm might include – height of plant, number of leaves, size of leaves, number of tomatoes, size of tomatoes, thickness of stem, amount of chlorophyll in the leaves (i.e. darkness of the green colouring), extent and pattern of roots.
■ *Activity 3.* Students work in small groups to measure the mass of a sample of tomatoes. All the tomatoes for a group should be of the same variety, and the sample should be as large as is practically possible. The data is recorded for interpretation in the plenary. Use a spreadsheet if possible.

■ *Activity 4 Answers:*
(a)

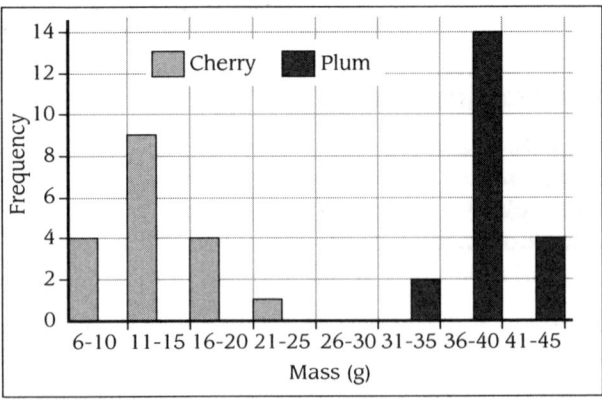

(b) The smallest mass of a cherry tomato is in the range 6–10 g.
(c) The largest mass of a cherry tomato is in the range 21–25 g.
(d) The range of masses for all the plum tomatoes is 31–45 g.
(e) Yes the scientist's prediction was correct. There is greater variation in mass between the two types of tomato than there is within either type. All the cherry tomatoes have a mass less than 26 g, and all the plum tomatoes have a mass greater than 30 g, without any overlap. Most cherry tomatoes have a mass between 11 g and 15 g, whereas most of plum tomatoes have a mass between 36 g and 40 g.

Plenary and homework suggestions

■ *Review 5.* Draw students' attention to Activity 4, which should support them. The results should demonstrate continuous variation.
■ *Review 6* Answers: chromosomes; genes; environment; light; soil; flavour; disease.

Differentiation/extension

■ *Starter.* Extend the more able by asking them to explain how each factor caused the variation.
■ *Activity 3.* Support lower ability students by providing a prepared spreadsheet or results table.

Technician notes
Activity 1. Variation in tomatoes
■ a few examples each of several different types of tomatoes, and tomato plants if available

Activity 3. Collecting data about tomatoes
Groups choose their tomato type.
■ several tomatoes of the same type
■ digital balance
■ spreadsheet access (optional)

⚠ Safety

Check for allergies to tomatoes. Students must not consume food in the laboratory.

Unit 1 - Inheritance and selection

Selective breeding

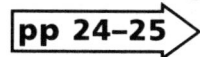

pp 24–25

Curriculum link

NC PoS: Sc2:4c
Framework: C3
QCA SoW: 9A Inheritance and Selection
Prior learning: 7B Reproduction

Students should know that sexual reproduction involves the fusion of the nucleus of the male sex cell with the nucleus of the female sex cell.

Be sensitive to the feelings of individuals and those of particular religious groups to the eating of meat and the rearing of animals as a human resource.

Lesson guidance

Starter suggestions

- Tell students that they must choose their own starting point for the paper chain on cross-pollination by insects. When they have written the first statement, they pass the paper to another student who writes down the next stage. This continues until the last student feels that the only statement that can be written is, 'Pollen deposited on stigma'. An example of a chain can be:
  Pollen produced by anthers → Insect arrives at flower to feed on pollen/nectar → Pollen sticks to insect's body → Insect flies to another flower → Pollen deposited on stigma.
- Afterwards, discuss whether everyone started at the same point, and the number of stages in each chain.

Development

- *Activity 1.* Examples the class brainstorm can elicit are: increase yields, tastier/more appealing colours/more appealing textures of food, more colourful/prettier/sweet-smelling flowers, produce medicines, produce materials for clothing, produce fuels etc.
- *Activity 2* Answer: large and tasty strawberries.
- *Activity 3, Worksheet 2* Answers:
  Q1 Less likely to blow over in the wind; less crop damage.
  Q2 A larger ear gives an increased yield of grain.
  Q3 The diagram should show favoured features from both plants, i.e. many large flowers.
  Q4 Transfer the pollen from the anther of one plant onto the stigma of the other.
  Q5 New varieties of colour, smell, texture of petal, disease resistance etc.
- *Activity 4* employs the twos-to-fours discussion technique, with pairs sharing their ideas with another pair before class feedback and discussion.

Plenary and homework suggestions

- *Review 5, Worksheet 3* Answers:
  Q1 Suggestions might include: health, condition of coat, strength, muscle tone
  Q2 Increased muscle size (more beef meat), skin texture (better quality leather), increased resistance to disease etc.
  Q3 Mammals, which feed their young on milk, have a body covered in hair and give birth to live offspring.
- *Homework 6.* Answers should include the fact that the breeder would need to select over a number of generations.

Differentiation/extension

- *Activity 2 and Activity 3, Worksheet 2.* Lower ability students may benefit from seeing strawberry plants, wheat and roses to help them visualise the possibilities for variation.

Technician notes
Starter. Cross-pollination paper chain
- sheet of paper per student

Activity 2 and Worksheet 2. New varieties
- plants of strawberry, wheat and rose

Unit 1 – Inheritance and selection

Investigating selective breeding

pp 26–27

Curriculum link

NC PoS: Sc1:2a,2d,2e,2g–k
Framework: SE4–SE6
QCA SoW: 9A Inheritance and Selection
Prior learning: Students should understand the technique of sampling.

Lesson guidance

Starter suggestions

■ Ask pairs of students to draw a table with three columns on a whiteboard. They must try to remember which human characteristics belong in each category. For example:

Genetic	Environmental	Both
Hair colour	Accent	Height
Eye colour	Language spoken	Weight
Tongue rolling	Hair length	etc

Development

■ *Activity 1.* The aim is for students to practise phrasing investigation questions that involve a relationship between two variables. Suggestions for (a) might include: size, mass, colour, smoothness, taste, cooking time, shelf life. Questions for (b) might therefore be: Does the colour of peas affect the taste? Does the size of peas affect their shelf life? Does the smoothness of peas affect the mass?

■ *Activity 2. Worksheet 4.* The aim is for students to appreciate the importance of sample size in obtaining sufficient and reliable data in order to come to conclusions. If you do not have a balance sensitive enough to weigh individual peas, each sample will need to be measured together and averaged out. This provides the opportunity to discuss why averaging loses information about the variation between individual peas.
Q1. Help students to understand that when results are not exactly the same, the difference may be so small as to be insignificant.
Q2. Reinforce the fact that the larger the sample, the more reliable the results.
Q3. Encourage students to look closely at the data they have collected in order to help them to come to a conclusion.
Q4. This answer will depend on the amount of variation in the data.

■ *Activity 3.* Students should include the following in their conclusion:
A description of the positive relationship between the variables, e.g. As the mass of the potatoes increases, the time for them to cook increases. Figures from the graph to explain this description, e.g. Variety 1 potatoes are generally smaller than Variety 2, and range in mass from 20 g to 120 g. Correspondingly, the time to cook ranges from 300 s to 1400 s.
The shapes of the line graphs to describe the difference between the two varieties of potato, e.g. The slope of the graph for Variety 2 is less steep than for Variety 1, indicating that the increasing mass has a greater effect on the cooking time for Variety 1 potatoes.

Plenary and homework suggestions

■ *Review 4.* Students can use the information in Figure 3 and their conclusion to Activity 3 to help them to interpret their own data on Worksheet 4 and come to a conclusion.

■ *Homework 5.* Controlled factors for a fair test could include: conditions in which the plants were grown, e.g. nutrients in the soil, water, light, time from harvest; or test conditions, e.g. size of pan for boiling, volume of water in pan, temperature of cooker ring etc.

Differentiation/extension

■ Extend more able students by asking them to explain the meaning of 'GM crops', and to discuss the reasons for and against their development and use.

Technician notes
Activity 2. Investigating mass of peas
■ samples of fresh and frozen peas
■ digital balance

⚠ Safety

Check for allergies to food materials displayed. Students must not consume food in the laboratory.

Unit 1 - Inheritance and selection

Cloning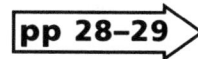

Curriculum link

NC PoS: Sc2:1d,4c; Sc1:1a
Framework: C3, SE1
QCA SoW: 9A Inheritance and Selection
Prior learning: 7A Cells

Students should remember how cells make copies of themselves.

Lesson guidance

Starter suggestions

- Show students a number of pictures of organisms (see Technician notes) for them to decide which method of reproduction applies. Students write 'asexual' and 'sexual' on each side of a whiteboard in order to display their answer.

Development

- *Activity 1.* It is always worth visiting the websites in advance of the lesson to check their suitability to your class. The *New Scientist* website has a useful section on Cloning FAQs and a Your Questions Answered section. Search the BBC and *Guardian* news sites for the latest on cloning.
- *Activity 2, Worksheet 5.* Students follow the instructions to grow plants from cuttings. Store them in a place with good light. Cuttings will not root if cold. Roots should appear in a week or two.
- *Activity 3.* The twos-to-fours discussion technique is suggested (see page 3). If time permits, summarise group findings with the whole class.

Plenary and homework suggestions

- *Review 4.* Answers:
  - (a) Blood group and hair colour
  - (b) Nucleus
  - (c) Sexual reproduction involves a male and a female parent because two nuclei, one from each of the sex cells, come together at fertilisation. By contrast, asexual reproduction involves only one parent and the cells make identical copies of themselves.
  - (d) 46 (human)
  - (e) clones
  - (f) Producing varieties that are more suited to our needs e.g. bigger yields, tastier food, cures for diseases, or any other suitable advantage.
  - (g) It reduces genetic variety and could put breeds at risk of extinction.

Differentiation/extension

- *Activity 1.* Support lower ability students either by giving them specific questions to find the answers to on the websites, or by displaying the websites with a data projector so that you can go through the information with them.
- *Activity 3.* Support lower ability students by pairing them with a more able student for the discussion. The more able will be extended when they join with another group to continue the discussion.

Technician notes
Starter. Pictures of organisms
Examples for asexual reproduction:
- bacteria, stick insect, amoeba, yeast, potato

Examples for sexual reproduction:
- rose, butterfly, frog, seagull, dog

Worksheet 5. Growing cuttings
- parent plant, e.g. geranium, begonia or tomato plant
- scissors
- conical flask
- cotton wool
- plant pot, soil and compost

⚠ Safety

Worksheet 5. Check for student allergies.

Unit 2 – Fit and healthy

A fit body 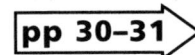 pp 30–31   WS 6

Curriculum link

NC PoS: Sc2:2n; Sc1:2g,2i
Framework: C2, SE5
QCA SoW: 9B Fit and Healthy
Prior learning: 7A Cells, 7B Reproduction, 8A Food and Digestion, 8B Respiration, 8C Microbes and Disease

Lesson guidance

Starter suggestions

■ Answers to the crossword:
1. Physical activity = exercise
2 across. Hooked on a drug = addicted
2 down. A poisonous liquid that should only be drunk in small amounts = alcohol
3. A healthy one is balanced = diet
4. Breathing in the smoke from burning leaves wrapped in paper = smoking

Development

■ Students should realise the connections between the different organ systems of the body as they read through the information in the table. Draw together their previous knowledge (see Prior learning) and apply it to this new concept.

■ ⚠ *Activity 1, Worksheet 6.* Students measure various aspects of their fitness. The squat jumps and running on the spot require adequate space to avoid injury. Students may need help finding their pulse; make sure they do not use their thumb as this has its own pulse. When students hold the 1 kg masses, they must stand up straight and pull in their stomach to avoid any back injuries. Similarly, when returning to the vertical position after bending forward, the stomach should be pulled in. For your information, the faster the breathing and heart rates, the less fit a person is. Resting heart rate averages at 70 bpm (beats per minute) for an adult, with children tending to be slightly higher. The picture of the glass is the classic optimist/pessimist description of half full or half empty. Students may need support on the best way to display and interpret their data.

Plenary and homework suggestions

■ *Review 2.* Students should include the following suggestions:
Stephen – Stop smoking; have a more balanced diet with less fat and more fruit and vegetables; take regular exercise and be sure to get enough sleep.
Carol – Reduce alcohol intake; maintain regular exercise.

Gary – Check that the diet is balanced and contains all the essential nutrients; take more regular exercise.

■ *Homework 3.* Students consolidate what they have learnt as well as gathering information to help them gauge their types of fitness.

Differentiation/extension

■ *Review 2.* More able students can extend the work further by describing the most suitable type of exercise for their chosen person.

■ *Homework 3.* For less able students, provide a table to complete with their activities during the day which they can then number from 1 for most strenuous, down to the least.

Technician notes
Worksheet 6. Measuring fitness
■ suitable space, e.g. gym
■ stopwatch
■ 1 kg mass
■ 30 cm rule

⚠ Safety

Ensure the students carry out the activities in a suitable wide-open space, and that they work safely to avoid injuries. Be aware of asthmatics and students with disabilities or chest infections.

Unit 2 – Fit and healthy

Breathing for oxygen

pp 32–33

Curriculum link

NC PoS: Sc2:2i–l
Framework: C1, C2
QCA SoW: 9B Fit and Healthy
Prior learning: 7A Cells, 7B Reproduction, 8A Food and Digestion, 8B Respiration, 8C Microbes and Disease

Students should be able to name the gases that are exchanged in the alveoli.

Lesson guidance

Starter suggestions

■ Use this exercise in labelling an alveolus and capillary to gauge how much students have remembered from the Respiration topic in Student Book 2, and the extent to which they need to review respiration before continuing with this lesson.

Development

■ *Activity 1.* Demonstrate ventilation, using bell jar lungs. Show how increasing the volume inside the jar causes the balloons to inflate. Relate this to the movement of the rib cage and the diaphragm, and show the students where to position their hands to feel this movement during breathing. Discuss the similarities and differences between this model and the chest and its action.

■ *Activity 2* Answer:

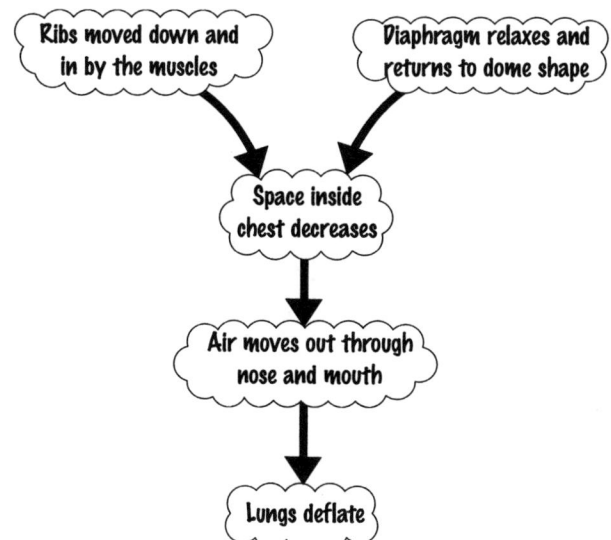

■ *Activity 3* Answers:
(a) Food is broken down physically by chewing, and then churning in the stomach. Enzymes break down carbohydrates chemically to glucose. The glucose molecules are small enough to pass through the wall of the small intestine without enzyme action.
(b) Oxygen and glucose are transported in the bloodstream, which is forced around the body by the contractions of the heart.
(c) Carbon dioxide and water.
(d) Glucose + oxygen
$\rightarrow$ (ENERGY +) carbon dioxide + water
$C_6H_{12}O_6 + 6O_2 \rightarrow 6CO_2 + 6H_2O$

■ *Activity 4, Worksheet 7* Answers: 1 contract, 2 swollen, 3 narrows, 4 faster, 5 relaxes, 6 air, 7 rate.

Plenary and homework suggestions

■ *Review 5.* This activity links back to the Respiration topic in Student Book 2. Answers: Both use up oxygen and release carbon dioxide; both release stored chemical energy; both are chemical reactions.

Differentiation/extension

■ *Starter.* If available, show students some images of alveoli and their surrounding capillaries that illustrate their three-dimensional arrangement.

■ *Activity 1.* Extend more able students by explaining that the movement of the air in and out of the lungs happens due to the *difference* in air pressure inside and outside the chest.

Technician notes
Activity 1. Bell jar lungs demonstration
■ bell jar
■ rubber bung
■ thick rubber base, e.g. a cut football, with string pull
■ 2 balloons attached to glass tubes
Assemble the apparatus as shown:

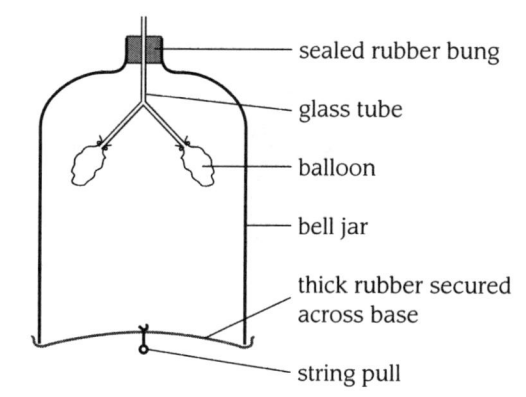

Unit 2 – Fit and healthy

The effects of smoking and drugs pp 34–35   WS 8

Curriculum link

NC PoS: Sc2:2i,2m; Sc1:1a,2i
Framework: C2, SE1
QCA SoW: 9B Fit and Healthy
Prior learning: 7A Cells, 7B Reproduction, 8A Food and Digestion, 8B Respiration, 8C Microbes and Disease

Be sensitive to any students who may have had problems or diseases in their family due to drug abuse.

Lesson guidance

Starter suggestions

■ Check that students understand the definition of a drug in the Starter, then read this list: coffee, paracetamol, cough syrup, glue, nail polish remover, hairspray, heroin, aspirin, tobacco, Coca-Cola, opium, LSD, cannabis, amphetamine, tranquilliser, cocaine, alcohol.

Development

■ *Activity 1* should be carried out in a fume cupboard or a well ventilated room, with asthmatics near an open window or door. Demonstrate the amount of tar from burning one cigarette and explain how it stains people's fingers and teeth as well as damaging the lungs. If you are using a fume cupboard, compare a filter cigarette with a non-filter one.

■ *Activity 2* Answers:
(a)

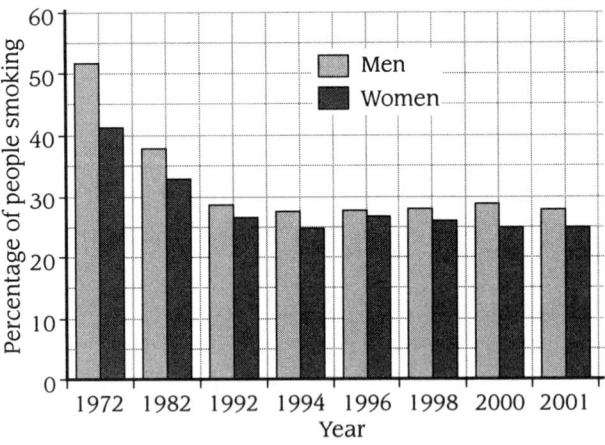

(b) Possible reasons: increased knowledge and education about the effects of smoking on people's health; increased cost (of cigarettes and health/medical/life insurance); increase in the number of public areas where smoking is banned.

(c) Suggestions should include promoting ideas of improved health and saving money.

■ *Activity 3.* Carefully select websites suitable for your students. Each small group researches its allocated drug. Read out the homework and ask groups to collect information for preparing the homework leaflet. Groups can present the Activity 3 information using *PowerPoint* or a poster. Copy the mind map of Figure 5 onto the board and add the information the groups have found.

Plenary and homework suggestions

■ *Review 4, Worksheet 8* Answers: Caffeine D, Nicotine C, Amphetamine G, Alcohol H, Cocaine A, LSD E, Cannabis B, Heroin F.

■ *Homework 5.* Ask students to use what they have learnt to produce an informative and persuasive leaflet.
Encourage the use of ICT in the production of an interesting design.

Differentiation/extension

■ *Starter.* Explain to more able students that the definition of a drug is actually quite difficult, as even substances like water and vitamins have effects on the functioning of the body.

■ *Activity 3.* Support lower ability students by providing them with a list of websites and particular questions to find the answers to.

Technician notes
Starter
■ whiteboards and pens

Activity 1. Smoking demonstration
■ U-tube containing cotton wool or mineral wool
■ rubber bungs and rubber tubing attachments
■ valve attachment to water tap
■ cigarettes, with and without filter
Assemble the apparatus shown:

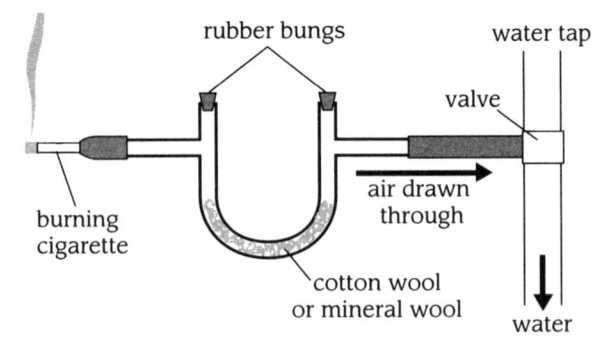

Activity 2. Bar chart
■ graph paper

Activity 3. Drug research
■ access to internet and/or school library

⚠ Safety

Activity 1 should be carried out in a fume cupboard if possible, or in a well ventilated room. Position asthmatics near an open window or door.

Unit 2 – Fit and healthy

Finding a balance

pp 36–37 ➤ WS 9

Curriculum link

NC PoS: Sc2:2a,2e; Sc1:1a–c
Framework: C2, SE1–SE3
QCA SoW: 9B Fit and Healthy
Prior learning: 7A Cells, 7B Reproduction, 8A Food and Digestion, 8B Respiration, 8C Microbes and Disease

Students should know that a balanced diet is required for health, and be able to name the constituents of a balanced diet.

Lesson guidance

Starter suggestions
- Answers: carbohydrates, fats, fibre, water, protein, calcium, vitamin C.

Development
- *Activity 1*. Use 2 cm³ of vitamin C solution of known concentration. Add drop by drop to 2 cm³ of 0.1% of DCPIP (PIDCP) until the blue colour clears, noting the volume of vitamin C solution required. Students should conclude that the greater the volume of juice required for a colour change, the less vitamin C it contains.
- *Activity 2*. Display the researched information as a time line. As a guide:
  18th century – *Dr Lind* of the British navy found that eating lemons and oranges prevented scurvy.
  19th century – *Admiral Takaki* realised that adding vegetables and meat to the diet of the Japanese navy cured the disease beri-beri. Until then, sailors eating rice meals every day suffered limb paralysis and could not fight. *Dr. Eijkman*, a Dutchman, sought the cause of beri-beri, which he thought was a type of microbe. He gave his assistant money to feed chickens well, yet many suffered from beri-beri. Then he found out that the man was stealing the money. Once the chickens had a proper diet, they recovered. In England, *Gowland Hopkins* discovered vitamins. *Françoise Magendie* demonstrated the importance of protein in the mammalian diet.
- Try: **www.hbci.com/~wenonah/new/howfindv www.medical-library.net/sites/_history_of_vitamins www.molecularexpressions.com/vitamins/pages/ vitaminc**
- *Activity 3, Worksheet 9*. In pairs, students can rehearse the proposed method using a metre rule. Students will benefit from the investigation planning sheets from Teaching Resource Book 1. Answers: Q1 Quantity of alcohol drunk. Q2 Reaction time. Q3 Does increasing the quantity of alcohol drunk increase reaction time?

Q4 Opportunity to discuss controlling variables for a fair test, and situations when this is difficult to do.
Q5 Measure reaction time before alcohol is drunk, and again after e.g. 1, 2, 3, 4, 5 half pints of beer.
Q6 Subjects must not have a medical problem or be taking medication affected by alcohol. The total quantity drunk should not be toxic. Use a safe area free of dangerous equipment or machinery. Subjects must sober up thoroughly before leaving.
Q7 The thumb and forefinger must be positioned at zero and the reading taken in centimetres exactly where the thumb touches the ruler.
Q8 Five values for the independent variable is enough, with a control of no alcohol at the start for comparison.
Q9 The larger the sample, the more reliable and representative the results will be. The number tested at any one time must be realistic.
Q10 Same: ruler, seating and catching position, hand to catch with, type of alcohol, quantity of alcohol for each drink etc.
Qs11, 12 Predictions should describe the relationship, i.e. increasing the independent variable causes the dependent variable to increase. Students should use their findings on the effects of alcohol to explain their prediction.
Q13 Websites have reaction timers (similar to those for computer games); a computer can measure the time in milliseconds.

Plenary and homework suggestions
- *Review 4*. Responses can be shared with the class.

Differentiation/extension
- *Activity 2*. Support lower ability students with website addresses and questions to answer, e.g. date of birth, date of discovery; what they found out; what changes their discovery made.

Technician notes
Activity 1. Testing for vitamin C
- 2 cm³ of vitamin C solution
- small flask or beaker
- 0.1% 2,6-dichlorophenol indophenol (DCPIP), otherwise named phenol-indo-2,6-dichlorophenol (PIDCP)
- syringes
- range of juices e.g. orange, lemon, tomato, blackcurrant

Worksheet 9. Investigating reaction time
- metre rule

⚠ Safety

Activity 1. Students must not consume food in the laboratory. DCPIP has no known hazards.

Activity 3. Take care when dropping the rulers.

Unit 3 – Plants and photosynthesis

What is photosynthesis?

pp 38–39 ⟩

Curriculum link

NC PoS: Sc2:3a,3b
Framework: C4, C5, I1
QCA SoW: 9C Plants and Photosynthesis
Prior learning: 7D Variation and Classification, 7C Environment and Feeding Relationships

Students are likely to know that plants are classified together in a group. They should also know that roots take in water from the soil and that the leaf is important in photosynthesis.

Lesson guidance

Starter suggestions

■ Draw a food chain on the board and ask students to: (a) provide the labels such as producer/plant, primary consumer/herbivore, secondary consumer/carnivore, and (b) explain that energy levels decrease along the food chain because each organism uses some of the energy it acquired to keep it alive which means less is available for the next (trophic) level.

Development

■ *Activity 1* Answer: Carbon dioxide is a gas in the air and it enters the leaf through the stomata. Water soaks into the soil when it rains and is absorbed by the roots.

■ *Activity 2*. Allocate a scientist to each small group of students to research using secondary sources of information (books, internet, CD-ROMs). Their information can be displayed as a timeline in the classroom. As a guide for your information:
Aristotle (384–322BC) formed a hypothesis based on observation. Plants and animals die and then rot into the ground, so plants must use these materials in the soil to help them grow.
Van Helmont (1692) planted a willow tree in 90 kg of soil and left it to grow for 5 years, only adding water. The soil lost 56 g during this time but the tree gained 74 kg. He concluded from his experiment that the tree uses the water to grow and gain weight.
Joseph Priestley (1733–1809) showed in 1771 that a candle could continue to burn, or an animal could continue to breathe, if kept in a jar with a plant inside. He concluded that the plant must restore the air and purify it.

Jan Ingenhousz (1730–1799) developed Priestley's experiments by demonstrating that plants would only purify the air when they were kept in the light but, in the dark, they would make it impure again.

Julius Sachs (1832–1897) demonstrated through a range of experiments that plants need minerals from the soil to grow healthily. He used water culture techniques and set up controls in distilled water for comparison.

Plenary and homework suggestions

■ *Review 3, Worksheet 10* Answers:
Organ where photosynthesis takes place = Leaf
Absorb water – a raw material for photosynthesis = Roots
Where glucose is made = Leaf
Provides the light energy for the chemical reaction = Sun
Absorb carbon dioxide – a raw material for photosynthesis = Leaf
Where the oxygen goes that is made during photosynthesis = Air

■ 📖 *Review 4*. Students' replies should express the fact that plants do not, as is commonly thought, get their food from the soil. Students should also demonstrate what they have learnt about the process of photosynthesis. Use responses for formative assessment.

■ 📖 *Homework 5*. Students learn the meanings of the key words for this topic so that they can use them appropriately throughout the rest of the unit.

Differentiation/extension

■ *Starter*. Differentiate by using terminology that suits the ability of your group.
■ *Activity 2*. Support lower ability students by providing them with a list of websites and particular questions to find the answers to.
■ *Review 4*. Support student literacy needs by providing a writing frame or sentence stems to complete.

Technician notes
Activity 2. Research for the timeline
■ access to internet and/or school library

Unit 3 – Plants and photosynthesis

Leaves: the organs of photosynthesis

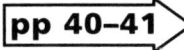 pp 40–41 WS 11

Curriculum link

NC PoS: Sc2:1b,1c,1e
Framework: C4
QCA SoW: 9C Plants and Photosynthesis
Prior learning: 7D Variation and Classification, 7C Environment and Feeding Relationships

Students should know the basic structure of a plant.

Lesson guidance

Starter suggestions

■ Use students' drawings of a plant cell to assess student recall and to gauge how much revision is required.

Development

■ *Activity 1.* Use a digital microscope and data projector to point out specific areas of leaf structure.
■ *Activity 2.* Thinly coat the underside of a leaf with clear nail varnish. When it is dry, use forceps to peel the varnish away and lay on a microscope slide with a coverslip on top. View with a light or digital microscope and data projector to see the imprint of the guard cells surrounding the stomata.
■ *Activity 3, Worksheet 11.* Students follow the instructions to test for the presence of starch in a leaf.
■ *Activity 4.* Answers:
(a) Part of leaf covered in black paper.

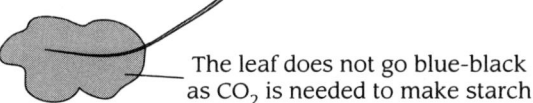

Blue-black colour indicates presence of starch.

Does not go blue-black as cannot produce starch in the dark.

(b) Soda lime which absorbs CO_2.

The leaf does not go blue-black as CO_2 is needed to make starch.

Control for (b) Sodium hydrogencarbonate to release CO_2.

All of the leaf goes blue-black as CO_2 was available to make starch.

(c) Variegated leaf.

Only the green part of the leaf goes blue-black as chlorophyll is needed to absorb sunlight for photosynthesis.

Plenary and homework suggestions

■ *Review 5* Answers: (a) A plant kept in the dark must use up its reserves of starch stored in the leaf. This means that any starch found in the leaf must have been produced under the conditions of the experiment. (b) The control is needed for comparison to show what happens when carbon dioxide is present.

Differentiation/extension

■ *Activity 2.* Extend the more able by comparing the number of stomata on the upper and lower surfaces of the leaf.

Technician notes

Activity 1. Viewing leaf sections
■ prepared microscope slides of leaf sections
■ microscope
■ digital microscope and data projector

Activity 2. Stomatal prints
■ clear nail varnish
■ plant with waxy leaves, e.g. Christmas cactus
■ microscope
■ microscope slide and coverslip
■ digital microscope and data projector

Activity 4. Testing leaves for starch
Goggles for each student
■ geranium leaf
■ 250 cm^3 beaker for water bath
■ Bunsen burner, tripod, gauze, mat
■ boiling tube
■ ethanol
■ forceps
■ white tile
■ iodine solution

⚠ Safety

■ *Activities 1 and 2.* Point out the risk from reflected sunlight when using daylight for mirror illumination with microscopes.
■ *Activity 4.* Safety spectacles must be worn.
⚠ Ethanol is flammable, so ensure Bunsen burners have been put away before issuing ethanol to the students. Warn them that iodine solution can stain their clothes.

Unit 3 – Plants and photosynthesis

The rate of photosynthesis

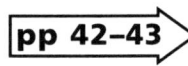

pp 42–43 → WS 12

Curriculum link

NC PoS: Sc2:3a, Sc1:2j,2k,2m–o
Framework: C4, SE3, SE6, SE7
QCA SoW: 9C Plants and Photosynthesis
Prior learning: 7D Variation and Classification, 7C Environment and Feeding Relationships

Students should be able to describe the structure of plants, identifying roots, stem, leaves and flowers. They need to remember that carbon dioxide is released from respiration.

Lesson guidance

Starter suggestions

- Photocopy each part of the word equation for photosynthesis onto separate pieces of paper and stick to the board. Give the class 2 minutes to decide how the words should be rearranged to form the equation before choosing student(s) to come forward to attempt it.

Development

- *Activity 1*. The apparatus should be set up as shown in Figure 1 of page 43 of the Student Book. The second experiment should be set up in exactly the same way but the light should be blocked, e.g. by wrapping the whole apparatus in black paper. After a set time, test for oxygen in both boiling tubes. The glowing splint should only relight in the experiment in the light.
- *Activity 2*. Answers:

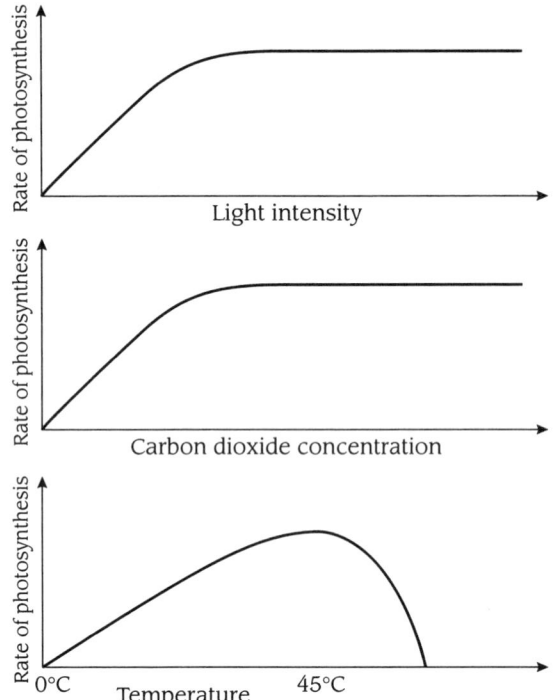

- *Activity 3, Worksheet 12*. Students can refer to the Investigation Support sheets on pages xv and xvi of this book to help them. Answers:
  Q1 Award marks for the correct scale and positioning of points.
  Q2 Number of bubbles decreases.
  Q3 Increasing the light intensity increases the rate of photosynthesis (or opposite).
  Q4 Number of oxygen bubbles would only increase by a small amount/not at all; rate of photosynthesis cannot be increased any further/has reached a maximum.
  Q5 Temperature in the water bath, volume of solution, lamp, type and size of pondweed, time to count bubbles etc.

Plenary and homework suggestions

- *Review 4* Answers: (a) carbon dioxide, (b) oxygen, (c) oxygen, (d) respiration, (e) the levels stay fairly constant as the carbon dioxide released during respiration is taken in by the plants during photosynthesis; similarly, the oxygen released during photosynthesis is taken in by all the organisms as they respire.
- ✏ *Homework 5*. The page students design for a website will be used in the next lesson.

Differentiation/extension

- *Homework 5*. Differentiate to match student ICT skills. Those who are confident and have computer access can design their web page using ICT, but give others the option of using paper.

Technician notes
Starter. Photosynthesis equation
Each section of the word equation for photosynthesis photocopied onto a separate large piece of paper:
- Water, +, +, Carbon dioxide, Sunlight, Chlorophyll, →, Glucose, Oxygen
- Blu-tack

Activity 1. Testing for oxygen from photosynthesis
- 2×25 cm³ beakers, each containing weak hydrogencarbonate solution
- $2 \times$ boiling tubes
- plasticine
- $2 \times$ glass funnels
- black paper or plastic
- $2 \times$ pondweed
- wooden splints

⚠ **Safety**

Activity 1. Wear safety spectacles when testing for oxygen.

Unit 3 – Plants and photosynthesis

Maximising plant growth

pp 44–45 WS 13

Curriculum link

NC PoS: Sc2:3c,3d, Sc1:2j,2k,2m
Framework: C4, SE6
QCA SoW: 9C Plants and Photosynthesis
Prior learning: 7D Variation and Classification, 7C Environment and Feeding Relationships

Students should know the best conditions to grow plants in, and that roots absorb water from the soil.

Lesson guidance

Starter suggestions

■ *Starter* Answers:
Flower = Reproductive organ – makes seeds
Leaf = Photosynthetic organ – makes glucose
Stem = Holds the plant upright and transports water, minerals and the products of photosynthesis to where they are needed in the plant
Roots = Anchor the plant into the ground and absorb water and minerals from the soil.

Development

■ *Activity 1.* Before they construct a mind map, explain to the students how to use symbols and pictures to represent text from the table, and to colour code appropriately.

■ 🐭 *Activity 2.* Prepare root squash slides in order to view the root hairs under the microscope. If possible, use a digital microscope and data projector to demonstrate this.

■ *Activity 3.* Set up a stick of celery in a beaker of food dye in advance of the lesson. Demonstrate the presence of the food dye in both the stem and the leaves, and slice a section of the celery stem to show the position of the xylem vessels.

■ 🖩 *Activity 4, Worksheet 13.* Students can refer to the Investigation Support sheets on pages xv and xvi of this book to help them. Answers:
Q1 (a) Plot 2, (b) Plot 3, (c) Plot 1.
Q2 (a) Plot 2 yield is in-between the other two, i.e. greater than without any fertiliser but not as much as when the nitrate level has been increased. Plot 3 has the biggest yield as nitrogen is needed to make proteins which are needed for growth. Plot 1, without any fertiliser, has the smallest yield.
Q3 Plot 1 is a control for comparison, i.e. comparing the yield without fertiliser to see what difference adding fertiliser makes.

Q4 An additional yield of 10.5 tonnes per hectare (2.5 times greater).
Q5 Crops are harvested. This means that the plants cannot die, decay and return the minerals they have used back to the soil. Fertilisers replace these lost minerals.
Q6 (extension question) Bacteria in the root nodules of peas and beans fix nitrogen back into the soil naturally.

Plenary and homework suggestions

■ *Review 5.* Students use the information learnt in this lesson to mark another student's homework produced in the previous lesson.

Differentiation/extension

■ *Activity 1.* Differentiate for the level of support needed.
■ *Activity 4, Worksheet 13.* Q6 is an extension question for the more able.
■ *Review 5.* Support lower ability students and extend the more able by pairing them up together for this activity.

Technician notes
Activity 2. Root squash slides
■ roots of garlic or cress
■ slide and coverslip
■ microscope
■ digital microscope and data projector

Activity 3. Demonstration
■ stick of celery with leaves still attached
■ beaker of coloured food dye
■ white tile and sharp knife

⚠ Safety

Activity 2. Take note of any student allergies. Point out the risk from reflected sunlight when using daylight for mirror illumination with microscopes. Students must not consume food in the laboratory.

Activity 3. Ensure the knife is stored safely. Again, note any student allergies, and ensure no food is consumed in the laboratory.

Unit 3 – Plants and photosynthesis

The products of photosynthesis

pp 46–47

Curriculum link

NC PoS: Sc2:3a,3b,3e, Sc1:2c
Framework: C1, C4, C5
QCA SoW: 9C Plants and Photosynthesis
Prior learning: 7D Variation and Classification, 7C Environment and Feeding Relationships

Students should know that respiration releases the gas carbon dioxide.

Lesson guidance

Starter suggestions

■ Re-use the words from the Starter on page 42 for students to rearrange into the correct equation. Extending this, students identify carbon dioxide and water as the reactants of photosynthesis, glucose and oxygen as the products, and chlorophyll absorbing sunlight as the conditions.

Development

■ *Activity 1*. Having written out the equations for respiration and photosynthesis, students should notice that they are the reverse of each other.

■ *Activity 2*. Students set up the apparatus as shown in Figure 2 on page 46 in the Student Book and make predictions on the colour of the hydrogencarbonate indicator in each boiling tube. Answers: In the light → purple as the carbon dioxide is used during photosynthesis; in the dark → yellow since photosynthesis cannot take place, and carbon dioxide increases due to respiration.

Plenary and homework suggestions

■ *Review 3, Worksheet 14*. Use for formative assessment of student understanding. Answers: carbon dioxide, stomata, roots, xylem, sunlight, carbon dioxide, water, glucose, oxygen, chloroplasts, palisade, respiration, producers, oxygen, water.

■ *Homework 4*. Students list at least five products from plants. Explain what this means, if students are unsure, but provide no examples at this stage.

Differentiation/extension

■ *Activity 1*. Extend the more able by providing them with the balanced chemical equations for photosynthesis and respiration.

■ *Review 3*. Extend the more able by removing the box of words from the worksheet so that they have to decide on the words themselves.

Technician notes

Starter. Photosynthesis equation

Each section of the word equation for photosynthesis photocopied onto a separate large piece of paper:

■ Water, +, +, Carbon dioxide, Sunlight, Chlorophyll, →, Glucose, Oxygen
■ Blu-tack

Activity 2. Photosynthesis happens in the light demonstration

■ 2 boiling tubes containing hydrogencarbonate indicator
■ 2 × pondweed
■ black paper or plastic
■ test tube rack

Unit 3 – Plants and photosynthesis

The importance of photosynthesis

pp 48–49 >

Curriculum link

NC PoS: Sc2:5a,5b,5e
Framework: I1–I3, C4, C5
QCA SoW: 9C Plants and Photosynthesis
Prior learning: 7D Variation and Classification,
7C Environment and Feeding Relationships

Lesson guidance

Starter suggestions

■ Put the word equation for either respiration or
photosynthesis on the board. Students need to
guess which equation it is and then rearrange it
to make the other.

Development

■ *Activity 1.* Follow up the homework from the
previous lesson by asking students to share their
lists of plant products. Show the class the stimulus
materials suggested in the Technician notes in
order to demonstrate the range of products.

■ *Activity 2* Answers:
Tube A = yellow – the snails release carbon
dioxide during respiration.
Tube B = purple – the plant uses up carbon
dioxide during photosynthesis.
Tube C = red/orange – the level of carbon dioxide
is the same as in the air.
Tube D = red/orange – the carbon dioxide
released during respiration is balanced by the
carbon dioxide used during photosynthesis.

Plenary and homework suggestions

■ *Review 3, Worksheet 15* can be used for formative
assessment of student understanding of the
importance of photosynthesis. Answers: 1 Light
energy; 2 Photosynthesis; 3 Glucose for food;
4 Oxygen for respiration; 5 Eaten by herbivores;
6 Eaten by carnivores; 7 Eaten by omnivores;
8 May form fossil fuels; 9 Carbon dioxide for
photosynthesis.

Technician notes
Activity 1. Stimulus materials
■ cotton wool
■ pasta
■ carrot
■ wood
■ vegetable oil
■ rice
■ nuts
■ paper etc

⚠ Safety

Activity 1. Students must not consume food in the
laboratory. Check for student allergies.

Unit 4 – Plants for food

Food production by plants

pp 50–51 →

WS 16

Curriculum link

NC PoS: Sc2:5e, Sc1:2j,2k
Framework: I1
QCA SoW: Unit 9D Plants for Food
Prior learning: 8D Ecological Relationships, 9C Plants and Photosynthesis

Students should know about the characteristics of life. There is the opportunity to revisit the meaning of a balanced diet. Be sensitive to the views of different people and religious groups towards the consumption of particular foods.

Lesson guidance

Starter suggestions

■ After students have worked on food chains, in pairs and then in fours, take class feedback and develop a food web on the board.

Development

■ *Activity 1.* Demonstrate examples of foods from plants (see Technician notes for suggestions) and ask students which organ of the plant they are or have been produced by. Check that students understand which are the four organs and can divide the foods into four piles – roots, stems, leaves, flowers.

■ *Activity 2.* Answers:
  (a) carbon dioxide + water $\xrightarrow[\text{chlorophyll}]{\text{sunlight}}$ glucose + oxygen
  (b) starch
  (c) They are a store of starch for energy when the plant is unable to photosynthesise; the plant survives underground when the physical conditions are unfavourable for growth.

■ *Activity 3.* Students will find that not all foods contain starch. This is because the glucose produced during photosynthesis can be converted to other substances.

Plenary and homework suggestions

■ *Review 4, Worksheet 16* Answers: Q1 99%; Q2 90%; Q3 (10% of 100kg =) 10 kg; Q4 movement, heat production, lost as waste urine and faeces; Q5 (10% of 10kg =) 1 kg.
Q6 Vegetarians are lower down the food chain and less energy has been lost; meat eaters are higher up the food chain and more energy has been lost by the herbivores using 90% of what they have eaten to stay alive.
Q7 Vegetarians must check their intake of protein, minerals and vitamins that are predominantly found in meat.

■ *Homework 5.* Having learnt the key words for this topic, students should be able to use them appropriately throughout the rest of the unit.

Differentiation/extension

■ *Activity 1.* Extend the more able by including examples that are less obvious, e.g. potato and ginger which are underground stems.

■ *Review 4, Worksheet 16.* Support lower ability students with their calculations.

Technician notes

Activity 1. Examples of foods
Formed from:
■ roots – carrot, parsnip
■ stem – celery, leek
■ leaf – cabbage, spinach
■ flower – cauliflower, broccoli, broad bean, tomato

Activity 3. Testing foods for starch
■ various foods from plants to test
■ iodine solution
■ white tile or spotting tile
■ pestle and mortar

⚠ Safety

Activity 3. Warn students that iodine solution can stain their clothes. Students must not consume food in the laboratory. Be aware of student allergies to particular foods.

Unit 4 – Plants for food

The effect of fertilisers on plant growth $\boxed{\text{pp 52–53}}$ ⟹ $\boxed{\text{WS 17}}$

Curriculum link

NC PoS: Sc2:3c, Sc1:2d,2e
Framework: C4, SE2, SE7
QCA SoW: 9D Plants for Food
Prior learning: 8D Ecological Relationships, 9C Plants and Photosynthesis

Lesson guidance

Starter suggestions
■ Help students to identify and understand the nutrients and minerals listed on the bottles or packets of fertilisers and plant growth foods that you display.

Development
■ *Activity 1.* Students are not expected to learn the function of each individual mineral at this stage, but just to appreciate that plants need a range for healthy growth.
Answers:
(a) Controls would be (i) in distilled water without any minerals added and (ii) with all the minerals for comparison.
(b) Same variety and age of plant; same volume of water; same quantities of each mineral; same amount of growing time.
(c) No conclusion can be made as there is a combination of symptoms which cannot be directly linked to the deficiency of one mineral.
■ *Activity 2, Worksheet 17* takes students through the planning process of an investigation. The Investigation Support sheets on pages xv and xvi of Teaching Resources Books 1, 2 and 3 can also be used to supplement this activity. If you intend to actually carry out the investigation, be aware that it will require 2–3 weeks for growth to take place and that some of the nitrate chemicals to be used as fertiliser are oxidising or harmful.
Answers:
Q1 The relationship investigated is what happens to the size of the plant population when the concentration of nitrate is increased.
Q2 Balance, measuring cylinder, water, beakers, duckweed, nitrate compound.
Q3 (a) At least 5 different concentrations to obtain sufficient results.
(b) Distilled water with no nitrate added, to compare the size of the population.
(c) For example: start with 10 in each beaker (total sample = 60 as there are 6 beakers, one for each nitrate concentration and one control beaker). Set up as many repeats/parallels as possible. Answers should indicate that larger samples give more reliable results.

(d) Volume of water, size of beaker, age of duckweed, time for population to grow, kept under the same conditions.
(e) Allergies; specific hazard from the nitrate compound.
Q4

Q5 Increasing the concentration of nitrate increases the size of the plant population. N.B. Accept any prediction provided it is substantiated by the answer to Q7.
Q6 Possible answers:

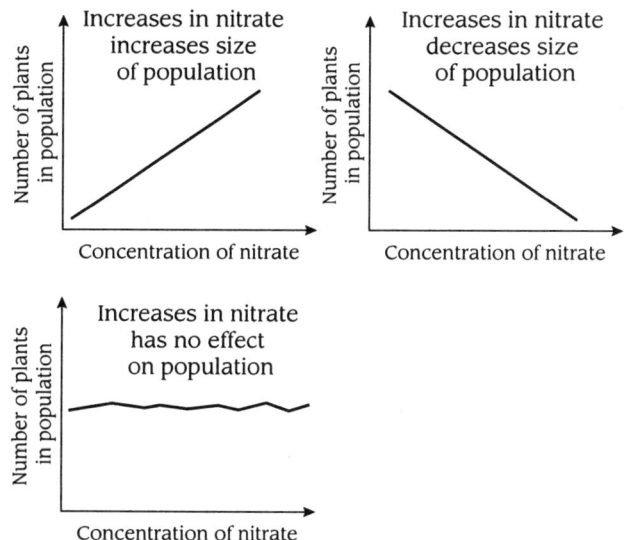

■ Q7 Nitrate is needed to make proteins, which are needed for growth. The duckweed can then reproduce and increase the size of its population.

Plenary and homework suggestions
■ *Review 3.* Students demonstrate what they have learnt about the effect of fertilisers on plant growth in their poster. Use the posters for formative assessment.

Differentiation/extension
■ *Review 3.* Differentiate by outcome.

Technician notes
Starter. Minerals in plant foods
■ empty bottles and packets of fertiliser and plant growth products

⚠ Safety

Starter. The bottles and packets should be washed thoroughly before display.

Unit 4 – Plants for food

Competition pp 54–55 WS 18

Curriculum link

NC PoS: Sc2:5d,5e, Sc1:2d,2e
Framework: I1, I2, SE2, SE4
QCA SoW: 9D Plants for Food
Prior learning: 8D Ecological Relationships, 9C Plants and Photosynthesis

Students should be reminded of how to use quadrats for sampling plant populations.

Lesson guidance

Starter suggestions

■ The mind map is developed as students make suggestions, and should include the following as resources that plants compete for: water, sunlight, minerals in the soil, space for root growth in the soil.

Development

■ *Activity 1.* Review the use of quadrat sampling from Student Book 2, page 52. Provide students with plant identification keys to establish which plants are weeds. Decide an appropriate sample size (aim for at least 10% of the field, or as much as time and resources allow) before using the quadrats to estimate the percentage weed cover of the whole school field.

■ *Activity 2.* Examples of animal pests might include: rabbits, aphids (greenflies), whitefly, slugs, mice, locusts etc.

■ *Activity 3.* Ideas from the discussion may include the following:

Technique	Advantages	Disadvantages
Hunt and kill each animal individually	Harms no other organisms	Time-consuming
Introduce or increase the animals that are the natural predators of the pest	Once the predator has been introduced, no further work is needed	May unbalance the food web
Use chemicals that are toxic to the pests	Quick and easy	May poison other organisms

■ *Activity 4, Worksheet 18.* In using the information provided to draw pyramids of numbers, students must also consider the effects of reduced competition when they redraw the pyramids. Use this exercise for formative assessment. Answers: The actual sizes of each box are not important, only the relative size within the food chain.

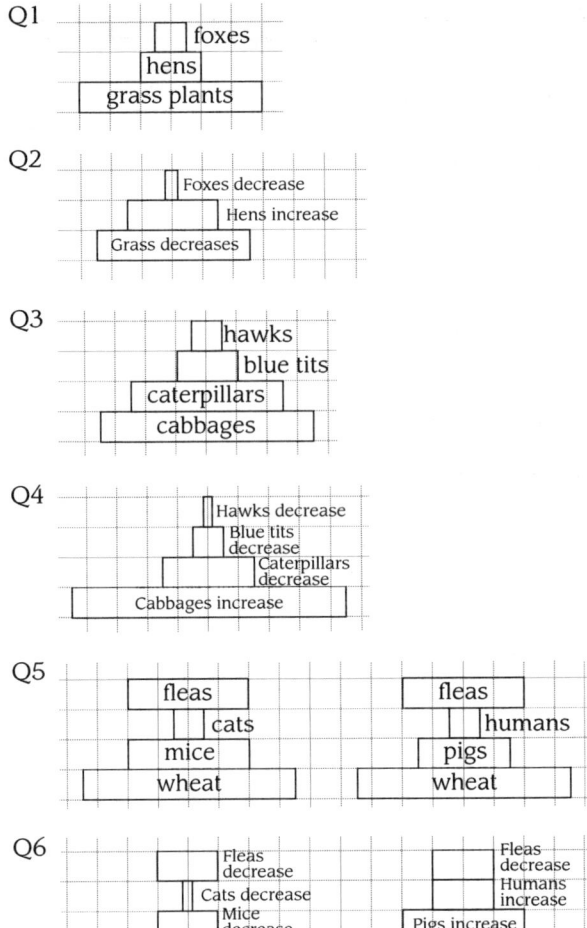

Plenary and homework suggestions

■ *Review 5.* Answers: crop, weeds, compete, water, soil, pests, web.

Differentiation/extension

■ *Activity 4.* Support lower ability students by asking them to answer Qs 1, 3 and 5 first, and then discussing Q2 before they draw this pyramid of numbers. They can then attempt Q4 on their own and, based on their progress, you can decide whether or not to omit Q6.

Technician notes
Activity 1. Sampling with quadrats
■ quadrat
■ plant identification key
■ quadrat record sheets for recording data

⚠ Safety

Activity 1. All off-site visits must be carried out in accordance with specific health and safety guidelines. A risk assessment should be carried out. Students should wash their hands after working outside. Allergies to particular plants, and hay fever sufferers, must be considered.

Unit 4 – Plants for food

Balancing the environment

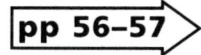

Curriculum link

NC PoS: Sc2:5a,5f
Framework: I1–I3
QCA SoW: 9D Plants for Food
Prior learning: 8D Ecological Relationships, 9C Plants and Photosynthesis

Lesson guidance

Starter suggestions
- The comments that students record on what they think growing food organically means will be used later in the lesson.

Development
- *Activity 1.* Students need to organise themselves into a food chain or web, with the number of students decreasing at each trophic level. Give each 'plant' a penny with the coins representing poison. The coins are passed on to successive trophic levels, and the further students are along the food chain, the more coins they receive. Continue this through the food chain to demonstrate bioaccumulation.
- *Activity 2, Worksheet 19* Answers: Q1 Osprey.
  Q2

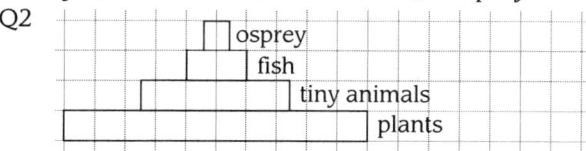

  Q3 6 g.
  Q4 Grebes and herons are higher up the food chain, so the DDT is more concentrated due to bioaccumulation.
  Q5 Two times greater.
  Q6 The sparrowhawks are higher up the food chain than the woodpigeons.
  Q7 Thin-shelled eggs are more easily broken if stood on or sat on.
- *Activity 3.* Return to the definitions of 'organic' that students generated in the Starter activity, and discuss as a class in order to decide on the best. This should include a reference to being produced without the use of artificial fertilisers or pesticides.

Plenary and homework suggestions
- *Review 4* Answers:
  (a) Producers are plants that make their own food by photosynthesis; consumers eat other organisms to gain their energy.
  (b) Iodine solution changes to a blue-black colour in the presence of starch.
  (c) Selective weedkillers are toxic to specific weeds rather than all plants generally.

(d) When one large organism can provide many consumers with energy and supports a larger population than its own.
(e) The pellets contain small quantities of the poison, passed on to the slugs. If small birds eat them, the birds will eat more than one and the level of poison will increase in their bodies. A bird of prey will eat many small birds containing the poison, and bioaccumulation takes place. The poison can reach toxic levels in the bird of prey, i.e. enough to kill it.

Differentiation/extension
- *Activity 1.* Lower ability students can represent a food chain only, but the more able can progress to a food web.

Technician notes
Starter. Meaning of 'organic' food
- packets and examples of foods grown organically

Activity 1. Demonstration of bioaccumulation
- penny coins

⚠ Safety

Starter. Students must not consume food in the laboratory.

Unit 5 – Reactions of metals and metal compounds

Properties of metals

pp 58–59 ⟹ WS 20

Curriculum link

NC PoS: Sc1, Sc3
Framework: SE1, SE5
QCA SoW: 9E Reactions of Metals and Metal Compounds
Prior learning: 8E Atoms and Elements, 8F Compounds and Mixtures

Lesson guidance

Starter suggestions

Run as a brainstorm activity, and write ideas like 'metals are shiny', 'feel cold' etc. on the board. During discussion, familiarise students with the word 'property' by repeated use in context.

Development

■ *Demonstrate a bulb and battery conductivity tester.* Ask students to predict whether or not the bulb will light when testing wires of different metals and non-metals.

■ *Activity 1* Answers:
   (a) Agree *but...* or Disagree because... All have some common properties (give examples) *but* metal properties vary between metals (with examples).
   (b) Disagree – very broad range of properties (with examples).
   (c) Agree, the bulb will light – but the exception is graphite.

■ *Activity 3, Worksheet 20.* 'Metals and non-metals' can be carried out after the students have worked through Activity 1. Students may need help to remember how to make a conductivity tester. Focus discussion on why covering metals with paint or plastic stops the bulb from lighting. Answer: Q1 Graphite conducts electricity.

■ *Activity 2* Sample answers: Aluminium conducts electricity and is light, lithium is very reactive, iron is strong and cheap, gold is rare, very attractive and does not corrode.

■ The second half of Worksheet 20, 'Looking closely at metals', can follow Activity 2. Discuss the materials used in packaging as a technological development to support ideas in SE1. An important outcome is that 'foil fresh' packaging is actually a thin layer of metallised paint sandwiched in between plastic layers. Encourage students to think about why manufacturers make packaging *look* like metal when it is not. Focus too on the fact that the

high thermal conductivity of metals make them a good choice for oven-baking foods. Answers: Q2 (a) Copper is a better conductor, but aluminium is lighter and does not corrode. (b) Silver is a better conductor than copper and aluminium, but is too expensive to use. (c) Lithium has a very low melting point, is too soft and is explosively reactive. (d) Aluminium is lighter and resists corrosion, although it has a lower melting point. (e) Although iron does not always have the best properties, it is by far the cheapest available metal.

■ For information: 'Tin' cans are made from tin-coated iron, 'foil' is aluminium. Students may be interested to know that plastic 'foil' crisp packets are the main contaminant that people put into metal recycling schemes.

Plenary and homework suggestions

■ *Review 4.* Write the two sentences in huge speech bubbles against cartoon faces on the board, and add the points that the student make.

■ *Homework 5.* Encourage students to try to find out some technical information about their bikes – what metals are used? What alloys? Why are particular metals chosen for the different parts?

Differentiation/extension

■ ✎ ▦ To support SE5, students can use Worksheet 20 information to produce bar charts of properties either manually or using a spreadsheet.

■ Students can also research the properties and uses of different metallic elements and produce posters using magazine and catalogue cut-outs. See 'Follow the mouse' for suggested websites.

Technician notes
Demonstration of conductivity testing
■ bulb, battery, leads, croc clips
■ wires and strips of metals and non-metals

Worksheet 20. Properties of metals
Metals and non-metals:
■ battery in holder or circuit board, leads, bulb
■ metal and non-metal wires and strips, each labelled with name, e.g. copper, iron, nickel, aluminium, sulphur block, carbon block, graphite rod, glass tube of air with graphite rods in bungs at each end and labelled 'nitrogen gas'
■ length of plastic-coated flex
■ access to painted metal, e.g. radiator
Looking closely at metals:
■ packaging: range of metal and metallised plastic packaging, e.g. aluminium pie plates, foil take-away containers, empty 'tin' cans, sheets of foil, plastic foiled crisp bags and cereal bags, foil sweet wrappers

Unit 5 – Reactions of metals and metal compounds

Acids and metals

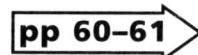 pp 60–61

Curriculum link

NC PoS: Sc3
Framework: P2–P4
QCA SoW: 9E Reactions of Metals and Metal Compounds
Prior learning: 8E Atoms and Elements,
8F Compounds and Mixtures, 7E Acids and Alkalis

Lesson guidance

Starter suggestions

■ Use outcomes from the student discussion to make a list on the board of 'good practice' rules for the safe handling of acids. This will feed into the practical activities of subsequent lessons.

Development

■ *Metals and sulphuric acid.* Demonstrate the reaction of magnesium and dilute sulphuric acid. Hold a bung on top of the test tube to allow the gas to build up, then 'pop' it with a lighted splint.

■ *Activity 1* Answers: hydrogen and magnesium sulphate; magnesium + sulphuric acid → hydrogen + magnesium sulphate.

■ *Activity 2* Answer: iron sulphate.

■ *Using different acids.* Students may notice that the formulae of nitrate and chloride salts sometimes show a '2' at the end. It is not expected that they understand combining powers at this stage.

■ *Activity 3,Worksheet 21* Answers:
Q1 The splint pops – hydrogen is made.
Q2 No more bubbles are seen.
Q3 The acid has been used up.
Q4 White solid is magnesium chloride.
Q5 (a) magnesium and hydrochloric acid,
(b) hydrogen and magnesium chloride,
(c) magnesium + hydrochloric acid → hydrogen + magnesium chloride, (d) hydrochloric acid and magnesium chloride (word equation if possible).
Focus discussion on the idea that the metal is 'using up' the acid to make the salt – this will feed into later development of ideas about neutralisation. Discussion with more able students can focus on the idea that the magnesium is gradually replacing the hydrogen atoms in the hydrochloric acid molecules until all the hydrogen has been 'kicked out' and none is left.

■ *Activity 4* Answers: (a) copper sulphate, sodium chloride, potassium nitrate, calcium sulphate. (b) sulphuric acid, hydrochloric acid, nitric acid, sulphuric acid.

Plenary and homework suggestions

■ *Review 5* Answers: (a) metal, hydrogen, (b) pops when lit, (c) sulphates, (d) hydrochloric.

Differentiation/extension

■ *Activities 1* and *3*. More able students should attempt writing formula equations for sulphuric and hydrochloric acid reactions. Less able students can be given cards showing the element or compound names and + and → symbols to arrange into equations.

Technician notes

Goggles for each student

Demonstration of magnesium and sulphuric acid reaction

■ magnesium ribbon pieces
■ sulphuric acid, 0.4 mol/dm³
■ test tube, bung
■ splint and Bunsen

Worksheet 21. Magnesium and hydrochloric acid

■ small pieces of magnesium ribbon
■ hydrochloric acid, 0.4 mol/dm³
■ test tube, bung and rack
■ splints and Bunsen
■ evaporating basin
■ gauze, tripod and mat

Formula equations for Activities 1 and 3 and Worksheet 21

■ cards, each with an element or compound name; + and → symbols

---

⚠ Safety

Goggles must be worn. Care should be taken when handling acids. Any splashes on skin should be rinsed immediately with water.

Unit 5 – Reactions of metals and metal compounds

Carbonates and oxides

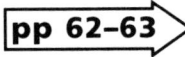

pp 62–63 WS 22

Curriculum link

NC PoS: Sc1,Sc3
Framework: P2, P3, SE4, SE5, SE7
QCA SoW: 9E Reactions of Metals and Metal Compounds
Prior learning: 8E Atoms and Elements, 8F Compounds and Mixtures

Lesson guidance

Starter suggestions
- Less able students can be given the answers on cards to link to the correct salt. Answers: magnesium and nitric acid, zinc and sulphuric acid, nickel and hydrochloric acid, calcium and hydrochloric acid. 'Uses' leads on from the previous lesson's homework on page 61 of the Student Book.

Development
- As a context for this lesson, discuss the erosion of building materials containing carbonates by acidic rainwater.
- *Activity 1* Answers: (a) calcium sulphate, (b) calcium nitrate (word equation if possible).
- *Activity 2* Answers: Key points – sulphuric acid reacts with calcium carbonate to make carbon dioxide, water and calcium sulphate (word equation if possible).
- *Activity 3* can be shown as a demonstration. Answer: The acid reacts to form calcium sulphate which forms an insoluble layer and protects the limestone from the rain, until it is worn off.
- *Adding copper to hydrochloric acid.* Demonstrate this before students start Worksheet 22, and make the point that metallic copper does not react with dilute acids – we make copper chloride from oxides and carbonates.
- *Activity 4, Worksheet 22.* Stress the importance of salts for making chemicals on a large scale to produce manufactured goods. Ask different groups to work with different solids – some with copper oxide, some with copper carbonate and some with malachite (if available). Make the point that copper salts for large-scale industrial use are made directly from ores like malachite. Show students how to assemble a filter, and remind them how to carry out evaporation safely. After the experiment, students should compare their own salt with other groups' samples, and with stock copper chloride. Discussion of this comparison supports SE7.

- *Worksheet 22* Answers: Q1 fizzing, solid dissolves, solution goes blue, beaker gets warm. Q2 copper oxide/carbonate + hydrochloric acid → [carbon dioxide (with carbonate only)] + copper chloride + water. Q3 Crystals are identical however they are made because they contain the same chemical compound.
- *Activity 5.* Show students iron tablets with 'ferric sulphate' on the label. Tell them that 'ferrum' is the old name for iron, hence 'Fe'. Answers: (a) sulphuric acid, (b) iron, iron oxide, iron carbonate.

Plenary and homework suggestions
- *Activity 6* Answers: metal carbonate + acid → metal salt + carbon dioxide + water
  metal oxide + acid → metal salt + water
- *Homework.* Ask students to learn the general equations for the reactions of metals, metal carbonates and metal oxides with acids.

Differentiation/extension
- *Activities 1* and *2.* More able students should construct full word equations. Alternatively, give more able students the formula equations and descriptions of reactions, and ask them to write word equations to match them.

Technician notes
Activity 3. Demonstrating the reaction of limestone and sulphuric acid
- sulphuric acid, 0.4 mol/dm³
- small lumps of limestone
- test tube

Worksheet 22. Making copper chloride
Demonstration:
- test tube, copper turnings, hydrochloric acid, 0.4 mol/dm³
Student groups:
Goggles for each student
- copper oxide, copper carbonate, malachite (or 'fake' malachite – copper carbonate mixed with sand)
- hydrochloric acid, 0.4 mol/dm³
- measuring cylinder, beaker, glass rod, spatula
- funnel and filter paper
- evaporating basin, gauze, tripod, mat
- access to 'stock bottle' of copper chloride (to look at only)

Iron tablets display
- empty bottle of iron tablets with label

⚠ **Safety**

Goggles must be worn. Copper salts are harmful. Splashes of acid or copper chloride on skin should be rinsed immediately.

Unit 5 – Reactions of metals and metal compounds

Neutralisation

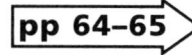 pp 64–65

Curriculum link

NC PoS: Sc3
Framework: P1–P3
QCA SoW: 9E Reactions of Metals and Metal Compounds
Prior learning: 8E Atoms and Elements, 8F Compounds and Mixtures

Lesson guidance

Starter suggestions

■ Alternatively, prepare cards for students showing the words and the definitions to match up. This is a preferable approach for less able students.

Development

■ *Activity 1* Answers: Metal carbonates, oxides and hydroxides all neutralise acids (bases) but only hydroxides are soluble (alkalis).

■ *Activity 2* Answers: (a) potassium hydroxide and sulphuric acid, (b) sodium hydroxide and nitric acid.

■ 🖱 *Activity 3*. Optionally, demonstrate adding alkali to an acid using a pH probe attached to a datalogger to show the sudden pH change at the end point. Show the results of the students' mixes and encourage them to make as many pH colours as possible.

■ *Activity 4, Worksheet 23*. Optionally, first demonstrate how a burette can be used to give very accurate readings. Discuss the idea of using a 'without indicator' repeat to make an uncontaminated salt sample. Students have practised evaporation several times, so a large evaporating apparatus on the teacher's bench can be used to save repeating this again.
🖩 Plenary discussion can compare the volumes measured by different groups. Focus on ideas of accuracy and the desirability of making repeats and taking averages to determine how much alkali to add.
Answers: Q2 (a) Not suitable for use in medicines. (b) Make very accurate measurement of neutralisation amounts, e.g. use of a pH probe, very clean or sterile equipment.

■ 📖📖 *Activity 5* can be extended into an exercise in writing style, e.g. making a list of procedures. Refer students to work from Year 7 on ideas of

diluting acid spill residues with water. Sodium hydroxide should not be used – any excess is harmful and would cause a further hazard.

Plenary and homework suggestions

■ *Review 6* Answers: (a) true, (b) false (e.g. metals), (c) false, (d) true, (e) false, (f) false.

Differentiation/extension

■ More able students can practise writing equations for other hydroxides with other acids. Also, give them names of salts and ask them to suggest reagents, equations and procedures for making them.

Technician notes

Goggles for each student

Activity 3. pH probe and datalogger demonstration
■ test tubes and rack
■ hydrochloric acid and sodium hydroxide, both 0.4 mol/dm^3
■ UI solution

For demonstration: Worksheet 23. Making sodium chloride
■ burette filled with sodium hydroxide solution
For student activity:
■ reagents as Activity 3
■ measuring cylinder, beaker, white tile
■ evaporating basin and heating apparatus (or large version on teacher's bench)

⚠ Safety

Goggles must be worn. Any splashes of acid or hydroxide on skin should be rinsed immediately with water.

Unit 6 – Patterns of reactivity

Metal reactions

pp 66–67

Curriculum link

NC PoS: Sc1, Sc3
Framework: P4, P5, SE6, SE7
QCA SoW: 9F Patterns of Reactivity
Prior learning: 8E Atoms and Elements, 8F Compounds and Mixtures, 9E Reactions of Metals and Metal Compounds

Lesson guidance

Starter suggestions

■ Remind students about the metals named in the starter panel: sodium and potassium fizz violently in water, magnesium is used for flares etc. Make the point that metals that react readily are found on the left side of the Periodic Table, slower reacting metals are usually over to the right.

Development

■ ✎ Show students samples of corroded metals. Demonstrate the fast tarnishing when sodium is cut with a scalpel. A low magnification digital microscope or camcorder attached via a PC to a projector can be used here. Introduce the term 'reactivity' as being a measure of how quickly metals react.

■ *Activity 1* Answer: sodium + oxygen → sodium oxide, silver + oxygen → silver oxide

■ Show a video or demonstrate the reaction of rice-grain size pieces of lithium and/or sodium and/or potassium in a trough of water with UI indicator. (Use a safety screen.) Discuss how reactivity increases down the group. See **www.chemsoc.org/viselements** for video downloads.

■ *Activity 2* Answers: rubidium, lower in group.

■ *Activity 3* Answer: Excludes air, water and light.

■ *Activity 4, Worksheet 24.* Keep the bottle of calcium with you – dispense it directly into the test tubes. Demonstrate how students should test for hydrogen. Magnesium will float since bubbles of hydrogen form on its surface – the surrounding UI will turn purple. Leave other tubes until next lesson. Show students how to set up the iron wool experiment by inverting a full test tube into the water – this can be 'doctored' by adding salt or a few drops of acid to the water after the students have left! Answers:
Q1 UI goes blue – alkali made, bubbles – gas.
Q2 hydrogen
Q3 calcium + water → calcium hydroxide + hydrogen

Q4 Use this task to support Sc1, SE6 and SE7, and refer students to the 'Draw conclusions' section of the Investigation Support sheets on pages xv and xvi in this book.
Luke's conclusion is consistent with his results, but he does not have enough *evidence* to *generalise* about the rest of the group. He needs to check *reliability* by repeating his experiment or checking with other students, and to carry out *further experiments* using other Group 2 metals.

Plenary and homework suggestions

■ *Review 5* Answers: Based on observed speed of reactions with air and water – sodium, magnesium, iron, silver, gold.

■ *Homework 6.* Students may find that wetter hinges etc. in bathrooms, kitchens and sheds corrode fastest.

Differentiation/extension

■ More able students should write word and possibly symbol equations for all reactions they see.

Technician notes
Display of corroded metal objects
See Teaching Resource 1 for Year 7, Acids and Metals, pages 19–20.

Demonstration of highly reactive metals
■ lithium and/or sodium and/or potassium
■ glass troughs, UI solution
■ tile, forceps, scalpel
■ safety screen
■ digital microscope and projector (optional)

Worksheet 24. Reacting metals with water
Goggles for each student
■ safety screen
■ calcium (with teacher), magnesium ribbon, copper turnings, iron filings, UI solution
■ forceps (to pick up calcium)
■ 5 test tubes, rack, bungs
■ splint, access to lighted Bunsen
■ beaker, iron wool, test tube

⚠ **Safety**

Goggles must be worn throughout. Use a safety screen for demonstrations. Calcium should be kept with the teacher.

Unit 6 – Patterns of reactivity

Acid reactions

pp 68–69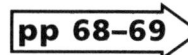

WS 25

Curriculum link

NC PoS: Sc3
Framework: P1, P3, P5, SE2–SE6
QCA SoW: 9F Patterns of Reactivity
Prior learning: 8E Atoms and Elements,
8F Compounds and Mixtures, 9E Reactions of Metals
and Metal Compounds

Lesson guidance

Starter suggestions

■ Warn students not to lose their hydrogen from
the iron wool experiment of worksheet 24! Show
students how to seal their test tube with a bung
while it is still inverted under water, and to test
the gas with a splint as soon as the bung is
removed. Students develop an order of reactivity
with water from these test tube experiments.
Introduce the idea that in this lesson they will be
finding whether or not this order is the same for
metals reacting with acids.

Development

■ The *Metals and acids* panel includes ideas covered
previously in the 'Metal Reactions' lesson. The
main new ideas to stress are that metals of
differing reactivities react differently with acids.

■ *Activity 1, Worksheet 25* gives students the
opportunity to practise skills in Sc1 and SE2–SE6.
They need to decide on the volume of acid to use,
and how they will either count bubbles or
measure temperature changes. They may find
that the bubble count they have chosen has to be
changed as they test less reactive metals:
encourage them to restart – this happens in 'real'
scientific research.
After testing with sulphuric acid (as a dibasic
acid, the reactions will be faster than for
hydrochloric acid) they can generalise about the
order of reactivity, but should realise that they do
not have enough evidence to predict the speed of
the reaction with other acids.

■ 📞 🖩 *Worksheet 25.* Students represent their
results in graphs using either graph paper or a
spreadsheet. Refer students to the Year 7
Investigation Support sheets on pages xv and xvi
of Teaching Resources Book 1.

■ *Activity 2* Answer: Silver does not react with dilute
acids.

■ The *Reactivity series* panel draws together ideas
covered so far. Explain to students that, in order
to react with acids, the metal must be able to
'kick the hydrogen out' to make the salt. Stress
the point that metals below hydrogen still
corrode by reacting with oxygen.

■ *Activity 3* Answers:
(a) Gold is very unreactive, iron has reacted
(rusted) in water and air.
(b) Copper does not react with water, but forms
copper oxide in air.

Plenary and homework suggestions

■ *Review 4.* Model this for students by suggesting
questions they could ask: 'Does it react with
acids? Does it react with acids faster than iron?'
Tell students that just asking 'Is it more
reactive/less reactive than…' is a forbidden
question (too easy!)

■ *Homework 6.* Copper is used for water pipes
because it does not dissolve in water (non-toxic),
is easily shaped and jointed, and does not react
with water.

Differentiation/extension

More able students should get as much practice as
possible at representing reactions using word
equations.

Technician notes
Starter
■ experiments from previous lesson – test tube
with bung, splint, access to lighted Bunsen

**Worksheet 25. How fast do different metals
react with acids?**
Goggles for each student
■ test tubes, rack, stopclock, thermometer
■ hydrochloric acid, 0.4 mol/dm³ similar sized
pieces where possible – magnesium, zinc, iron,
copper, lead
■ sulphuric acid, 0.4 mol/dm³
■ measuring cylinders

⚠ Safety

Goggles must be worn. Any acid splashes on skin
should be rinsed immediately.

Unit 6 – Patterns of reactivity

Displacement

pp 70–71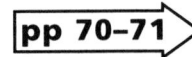
WS 26

Curriculum link

NC PoS: Sc1, Sc3
Framework: P1–P5, SE6
QCA SoW: 9F Patterns of Reactivity
Prior learning: 8E Atoms and Elements,
8F Compounds and Mixtures, 9E Reactions of Metals
and Metal Compounds

Lesson guidance

Starter suggestions

■ This could be worked in groups or by whole-class
discussion. Reacting metals with air, water or
acids would prove the order.

Development

■ The ideas in the *Displacement* panel can be
modelled using students holding signs: 'copper',
'zinc', 'iron', 'sulphate', 'chloride' etc. New salts
form when a metal and another salt 'hold hands'
in solution. Put a metal with a salt (look at the
reactivity series to work out which is 'more
reactive'); this one can 'grab' the
sulphate/chloride. Summarise using word
equations.

■ *Activity 1* Answers:
  (a) zinc + iron sulphate → iron + zinc sulphate
  (b) No, iron is less reactive than zinc.

■ *Activity 2* Answers: (a) yes, (b) yes, (c) yes.
  Aluminium is more reactive than zinc.
  (d) Aluminium and a magnesium salt solution.

■ *Activity 3, Worksheet 26.* Show students how to
use the table to work out which pairs of
substances to test. Tell them that 'no reaction' is
important in this experiment. Check that they
have all made predictions before they start. If
cost is an issue, these reactions can be carried
out using very small quantities on spotting tiles.
Answers:
Q1 magnesium + iron sulphate
                     → iron + magnesium sulphate
magnesium + zinc sulphate
                     → zinc + magnesium sulphate
magnesium + copper sulphate
                     → copper + magnesium sulphate
zinc + iron sulphate → iron + zinc sulphate
zinc + copper sulphate → copper + zinc sulphate
iron + copper sulphate → copper + iron sulphate.
Q2 Iron displaces copper because it is more
reactive.

■ *Activity 4* Answers:
  (a) aluminium + iron oxide
                     → iron + aluminium oxide
  (b) Different substances made, change not easily
  reversed, energy given out.

Plenary and homework suggestions

■ *Review 5.* Write pairs of metals and salts on the
board. Students hold up 'yes' or 'no' sheets to say
whether or not they think displacement occurs.
Pick students to name the products of the
reactions.

Differentiation/extension

■ *Activity 3.* More able students should attempt to
write formula equations for the 'sulphate'
reactions. Less able students can be given cards
with the names of the substances to arrange into
equations.

Technician notes
Worksheet 26. Looking at displacement
Goggles for each student
■ test tubes and rack
■ small pieces of copper, magnesium, zinc, iron
■ solutions of copper sulphate, zinc sulphate,
  magnesium chloride labelled 'magnesium
  sulphate' (approx. 0.4 mol/dm³), (acidified)
  iron(II) sulphate
■ 2 petri dishes
■ small iron objects, e.g. padlock keys, paperclips,
  nails or panel pins

⚠ Safety

Goggles must be worn. Any splashes of solutions
on skin should be rinsed immediately.

Unit 6 – Patterns of reactivity

Extracting metals

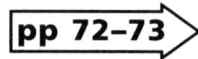 pp 72–73 WS 27

Curriculum link

NC PoS: Sc3
Framework: SE1, P4, P5
QCA SoW: 9F Patterns of Reactivity
Prior learning: 8E Atoms and Elements, 8F Compounds and Mixtures, 9E Reactions of Metals and Metal Compounds

Lesson guidance

Starter suggestions

■ Write 'Iron, Fe' and 'Iron oxide, Fe_2O_3' on the board. Use this as an example to show that making iron from iron oxide (e.g. haematite ore) involves making an element from a compound in a chemical change. Unusually, these reactions are endothermic – most changes students have met in the course so far are exothermic.

Development

■ If available, show videos of mineral extraction and processing. Stress to students that it is not only the availability and cost of extraction of the raw materials that makes metals expensive, but the high cost of energy in their processing.

■ *Activity 1* Answers: Electricity, needed to extract aluminium from its ore, was not available until about 150 years ago; the high cost of electricity makes aluminium expensive.

■ *Activity 2* Answer: Silver and gold are expensive because they are rare.

■ *Activity 3* Answers: Seating, dashboards etc.

■ 🖩 *Activity 4, Worksheet 27* asks students to think in terms of very large numbers. Answers:
Q1 Look for use of scale and accuracy of plotting.
Q2 World production is much higher, but the UK produces relatively high amounts of lead, copper, zinc and aluminium.
Q3 Iron production is so huge that it would not fit on the scale.
Q4 The more reactive, the higher the temperature needed.
Q5 Cost of fuel to reach 1600 °C too high.
Q6 Zinc, higher temperature requires more fuel.
Q7 Between iron and lead.
✍ 📖 Q8 Students can use the internet (e.g. **viselements** or **webelements** websites), books or CD-ROMs, and can present their findings in several ways. They can design posters, leaflets or talks. One possibility is making collages by bringing in magazine photos from home. Students could produce articles to make into a class magazine about metals.

Plenary and homework suggestions

■ *Review 5.* Ask students to complete the sentences orally by selecting the relevant facts from their books. Their responses can be used to make a summary of key points on the board.

■ *Homework 6.* Students can produce questionnaires to use on their family and friends.

Differentiation/extension

■ ✍ Students can carry out the tasks on Worksheet 27 using a spreadsheet.

■ More able students can research the chemical recycling of aluminium and discuss the economic and environmental issues relating to the process.

Unit 7 – Environmental chemistry

Soils

pp 74–75 ⟹

 WS 28

Curriculum link

NC PoS: Sc1, Sc3
Framework: SE1
QCA SoW: 9G Environmental Chemistry
Prior learning: 8G Rocks and Weathering,
9E Reactions of Metals and Metal Compounds

Lesson guidance

Starter suggestions

■ Produce a list on the board, e.g. examples of animal or plant waste and remains (dead leaves etc), small particles of rock and sand, live animals (worms) etc. Ways of classifying include 'from living things', i.e. organic matter, and 'non-living', i.e. inorganic. Students should realise that soil is being continually replenished – use this idea to revisit Year 8 work on sedimentation.

Development

■ Optionally, show students empty compost bags or visit a gardening website to see the contents of ericaceous and peat-free composts, and compare the advertisers' claims.

■ ▦ ◿ *Activity 1, Worksheet 28. 'Water content.'* Give students a map showing where the soil samples were collected. Different groups test different soils for water content. Samples can be dried quickly in a warm oven or left in a warm place until next lesson. Each group enters results in a table on the board or into a spreadsheet. If possible, show students where the soils were collected. Ask them to suggest reasons for differences in water content and to look for evidence that plants growing are different (e.g. plantains grow in dry bare places).

■ *Soil pH.* Show students a gardener's pH test kit. Answer: Q1 Soil mixture is too cloudy to see colours.

■ *Activity 2.* The destruction of peat bogs is of great environmental interest. Students can carry out internet searches to find out more information. Answers: (a) To grow acid-loving plants like heathers, camellias etc. (b) Peat bogs are non-renewable – the habitat will be destroyed, meaning extinction of plants and animals.

■ The *Farming and pH* panel does not discuss the fact that, for growth, plants need nutrients (either natural or in fertilisers), but students should be aware that other factors, not only pH, affect the healthy growth of crops.

■ *Activities 3* and *4*. Discuss how gardeners choose plants to suit their soil type, but farmers often have to change their soils to grow what is in demand or profitable.

■ *Activity 3* Answers: (a) Oats and turnips grow best, potatoes and beans will grow. (b) Lime the soil. (c) They like different pHs – soil in the same field will not suit both.

■ *Activity 4* Answers: True, turnips grow from pH 5.5 to 6.8; oats will grow, too.

Plenary and homework suggestions

■ *Review 5* Answers: (a) pH lower, more acidic. (b) pH higher, more alkaline. (c) To grow different plants.

■ *Homework 6.* An alternative homework suggestion is to look at gardening suppliers' websites to compare compost labels for advertisers' claims about performance and peat content.

Differentiation/extension

■ Students can do a project on the environmental issues surrounding the extraction of peat from peat bogs. Link this to the study of renewable energy resources in Sc4.

Technician notes
Types of soil
■ empty compost bags of different types
■ garden centre websites

Worksheet 28. Comparing soils
Water content (each group will test one soil)
■ about 6 samples of soils collected from different places around school, e.g. under hedge, beside path etc. – choose shaded and exposed areas (keep soils in sealed polythene bags; if necessary, create differences in water content by adding water to soils from shaded places)
■ sketch map drawn and photocopied, showing where samples have come from
■ metal food trays or shallow containers
■ access to warm oven (optional)
■ balance
Testing pH
■ soils as above, plus samples of compost (let students read labels) – at least one ericaceous and one 'peat-free'; if possible, soils from elsewhere of different pHs (or faked by mixing soil and compost)
■ test tubes, bungs, spatulas, pH paper and charts

⚠ Safety

A dressing or plastic gloves should be worn by any student with a cut or abrasion. Students should wash their hands after handling soils.

Unit 7 – Environmental chemistry

Acid rain

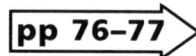 pp 76–77

Curriculum link

NC PoS: Sc1, Sc3
Framework: SE1, SE4, SE5
QCA SoW: 9G Environmental Chemistry
Prior learning: 8G Rocks and Weathering, 9E Reactions of Metals and Metal Compounds

Many students do not realise that rain is *naturally* acidic. Students often have vague notions about 'pollution'. Encourage them to be more precise in using the *names* of individual pollutant gases and their *effects*.

Lesson guidance

Starter suggestions

■ Ask groups to think about a portable acid rain test kit. Discuss the advantages of using electronic pH testers in environmental monitoring in terms of accuracy and storage of information. Students may have seen electronic boxes fixed to lampposts near busy roads to monitor and record levels of pollutant gases.

Development

■ *Activity 1* Answer: Rain has always been acidic due to naturally acidic gases, e.g. CO_2 from respiration and combustion.

■ *Activity 2* Answer: Burning of fossil fuels increases quantities of all three acidic gases in the air.

■ *Activity 3, Worksheet 29*. Help students to set up their apparatus to collect the gas. Use the results as an opportunity to practise drawing 'best fit' graphs. Students can use a spreadsheet to produce their graphs. Students may need help to recognise when to take readings. Stress that 1.5 min = 1:30 on the stopclock display.

■ As an extension, discuss that acid rain contains sulphuric acid and not hydrochloric acid. Show students that the reaction stops quickly if sulphuric acid is used. This is due to calcium sulphate, which is insoluble, forming on the limestone – see 'Carbonates and Oxides', page 62 of the Student Book. Answers:
Q1 Limestone chips left – acid is used up.
Q2 The smaller the size of lumps, the faster the reaction.
Q3 Detail on faces is similar to small lumps – these will react fastest with acid rain.

■ *Activity 4*. Students may find it helpful to look back at work on Fossil Fuels in the 'Simple Chemical Reactions' and 'Energy Resources' units from Year 7. This could be extended into a class debate.

Plenary and homework suggestions

■ *Review 5* can be a game between groups. Who can get the most answers? Who can come up with the most original answer?

■ *Homework 6*. Tell students that they need to think about choosing images to give a balanced view. They need to show not only the problems but how acid rain is produced, and the reasons why it is difficult to stop.

Differentiation/extension

■ Students can visit **www.airquality.co.uk** to find out about air quality in their own town.

■ *Problems caused by acid rain*. To illustrate the effects of acid rain, students could visit a graveyard to look at how older gravestones are not easily read due to the erosion of the stone. Tell them they should not touch any stones.

Technician notes

Worksheet 29. Acid rain and limestone
Carry out a trial run of the experiment and adjust concentration of acid so that the rate of collection of gas is appropriate to the size of measuring cylinder available.

Goggles for each student
■ 2 measuring cylinders, conical flask, bung and delivery tube, bowl, stopclock, access to balance
■ large limestone chips (or marble chips, labelled 'limestone'); small chips; powdered limestone (can use calcium carbonate)
■ hydrochloric acid, 0.4 mol/dm^3
■ sulphuric acid, 0.4 mol/dm^3 (for demonstration)
■ graph paper

⚠ Safety

Goggles must be worn. Any acid splashes on skin should be rinsed immediately.

Unit 7 – Environmental chemistry

Solving the acid rain problem pp 78–79

Curriculum link

NC PoS: Sc3
Framework: P1, P3
QCA SoW: 9G Environmental Chemistry
Prior learning: 8G Rocks and Weathering,
9E Reactions of Metals and Metal Compounds

Lesson guidance

Starter suggestions

- Students should think about the effects of the gases on health, e.g. asthma and breathing difficulties, as well as the 'acid rain' problems. They can look back at these ideas using the previous two pages in the Student Book. If there is room, the class could make a 'class scene' on the board, with each group taking turns to add a sketch to build up the scene. Keep this for the Review activity.

Development

- A key learning point for this lesson is that there are no 'magic' scientific solutions to pollution problems – all strategies have disadvantages as well as advantages. Scientists are part of a 'search for solutions' to environmental problems, and this is a developing science, e.g. adding limestone to lakes was carried out first, and we now have developing technologies to stop emissions.

- *Activity 1, Worksheet 30* can be extended into a more formal practice of 'fair testing' to extend Sc1 skills. Tell students that many gardeners collect eggshells to put around the soil near rose trees. Some students may have seen 'lime kilns' in the countryside. Answers: Q1 A new, different product has been made. Q2 Slaked lime.
  More able students may be able to follow word or formula equations for the reactions: on heating – limestone (calcium carbonate, $CaCO_3$) → calcium oxide (CaO) + carbon dioxide (CO_2), then add water so that calcium oxide (CaO) + water (H_2O) → slaked lime or calcium hydroxide ($Ca(OH)_2$).

- *Activity 2* Answer: The limestone gets used up, more acid rain falls.

- *Stopping acid rain from power stations.* Additional points for discussion: one of the key issues is that the quarrying of limestone creates its own environmental problems. Limestone scrubbers also produce huge quantities of calcium sulphate (gypsum) which can be used for making builder's plaster, but it is so expensive to produce that it is cheaper to landfill the waste. Longannet power station (Scotland) uses sea water scrubbers.

- *Activity 3* Answers: It will be cheaper in the long run. Also stops other effects, e.g. breathing difficulties, less waste of limestone/less resources used.

- *Activity 4* Answers: Cost of each, whether the power station is near the sea, transport links for raw materials.

Plenary and homework suggestions

- *Review 5.* These bubbles can be added to the class sketch, and should cover the key ideas from the Student Book pages.

- 📖 🖱 *Homework 6.* The students' research should raise discussion about how tackling one pollution issue often raises another.

Differentiation/extension

- There is an opportunity to revise ideas about acids reacting with carbonates here.

- More able students could write equations for limestone (calcium carbonate) reacting with sulphuric acid in acid rain.

- There is a wealth of opportunity for project work in this area.

Technician notes
Worksheet 30. Using limestone to neutralise acidic soil

If crucibles are not available, the limestone can be heated in evaporating basins or on 'tin' lids.

Goggles for each student

- 'limestone powder' (calcium carbonate)
- crucible, pipeclay triangle, watchglass, tripod, bunsen, mat, tongs, dropping pipettes, beaker of water
- test tubes and rack
- 'acid rain' – sulphuric acid, 0.4 mol/dm³
- broken eggshells, thoroughly washed
- UI solution and pH charts

⚠ Safety

Goggles must be worn. Warn students not to touch hot apparatus. After heating, the calcium oxide formed is corrosive – students should wash their hands after any contact with it.

Unit 7 – Environmental chemistry

Climate change

pp 80–81 ➤

Curriculum link

NC PoS: Sc1, Sc3
Framework: SE1, SE6, SE7
QCA SoW: 9G Environmental Chemistry
Prior learning: 8G Rocks and Weathering,
9E Reactions of Metals and Metal Compounds

Many students believe that heat from the Earth's surface is *reflected* back from greenhouse gases, like from a glass pane in a greenhouse (this is not helped by many textbook diagrams that imply this). This is incorrect – the gases absorb the heat, *retaining the energy in the atmosphere*.

Lesson guidance

Starter suggestions

■ Students have met ideas about fossil fuels in Years 7 and 8. Encourage them to think of our industrial dependence in addition to the obvious car fuel and central heating ideas – all our foods and consumer goods are made in factories using fossil fuel energy, as well as transportation to shops.

Development

■ *Activity 1* Answer: Earth would not be warm enough for life without it.
■ *Activity 2* Answers: (a) Predictions should be below –33 °C; actual temperature is –68 °C.
(b) Life depends on atmosphere for breathing etc. Too cold.
■ *Activity 3, Worksheet 31* builds Scientific Enquiry skills. For Q1, draw graph axes on the board to help students – remind them to use a linear scale for the years along the *x*-axis. The *y*-axis should start at 280 ppm and finish at 370 ppm.
■ *Worksheet 31* can be used in a variety of ways. See below for differentiation suggestions for different abilities. Students can carry out further research using websites (see 'Follow the mouse'), books or CD-ROMs) to prepare short presentations. (This is an area where frequent TV programmes are worth recording to show to students.) The presentations can either be by making posters, or magazine/newspaper articles, or by groups preparing OHTs to give a short talk.
The most difficult viewpoint to present is that climate change (the more up-to-date term for global warming) is not yet proved to be happening – this could be given to more able

groups. In particular, lead students to understand that data gathered over 100 years is very short term compared to the age of the Earth. Current research into past climates is by analysing air trapped in ice for millions of years, and the fossil record, e.g. tree rings.

■ *Activity 4*. Encourage students to think more broadly about the benefits of 'using less fuel'. This would save finite energy resources, and also lessen other polluting effects, e.g. acid rain. Students may also consider how technology is advancing so that cars and other engines are much more 'energy efficient'. They may also be aware that 'cutting CO_2 emissions' is a political issue, with governments across Europe agreeing targets to be met in the relatively short term. Answer: Use public transport, insulate houses, switch off unused electrical appliances, walk to school etc.

Plenary and homework suggestions

■ *Review 5* Answers. Advantages – Life would not have evolved without it; makes Earth temperature warm enough for life. Disadvantages – May threaten life/crops/animals, sea level rise, climate change.

Differentiation/extension

■ The websites suggested in 'Follow the mouse' contain very comprehensive information that could form the basis for extended research or topic work.
■ Less able students could be asked to work as a group to produce a series of linked posters, each one making a single important point about climate change.

Technician notes
Worksheet 31. Evidence that climate change is happening

■ either poster paper/pens or OHP, OHTs and pens
■ internet access, CD-ROMs, reference books about climate change/global warming
■ video/DVDs about climate change/global warming

Unit 8 – Using chemistry

Energy from fuels

pp 82–83 ➤

Curriculum link

NC PoS: Sc1, Sc3
QCA SoW: 9H Using Chemistry
Framework: SE2, SE4, SE5
Prior learning: 9E Reactions of Metals and Metal Compounds, 9F Patterns of Reactivity

Lesson guidance

Starter suggestions

■ One fuel (e.g. natural gas) could be used to construct a spider diagram of ideas on the board.

Development

■ Stress the idea that different fuels are 'ideal' for different purposes, and that our choice of fuels is governed by the technology that is available, e.g. widely available central heating boilers are all based on oil- or gas-burning technology.

■ *Activity 1* Answers: (a) Methane is non-renewable, fossil fuels are running out/greenhouse gas argument. (b) Most electricity is generated from fossil fuels – disadvantages as for (a).

■ *Activity 2* Answers: Advantages – petrol reasonably priced, available at every garage, does not leave solid waste when it burns. Disadvantages – non-renewable, gives out polluting gases.

■ *Activity 3, Worksheet 32* is a hazardous activity, so carry out a full risk assessment. Introduce the idea of camping stoves. Show students a 'butane'-type stove – you can boil a kettle of water and make a mug of tea as the lesson progresses. Show students how to use their apparatus safely: fuels burning in the lid are extinguished by covering them with a heatproof mat to exclude oxygen. Any accidental larger fires are extinguished using a wet cloth. Students should burn very small quantities of fuel, lighting them using spills. Liquid fuels can be burned in burners or in tiny quantities in crucibles. They will need to use a fresh boiling tube each time. Each working group should be limited to testing three or four fuels – the room will get very smoky!

Students need to think about *fair testing*. Refer them to the 'Fair test' and 'Presenting the data' sections of the Investigation Support sheets on pages xv and xvi of Teaching Resources Book 2. Suitable ideas include measuring temperature changes across a fixed time interval, or timing how long it takes to reach a fixed temperature change. It is not intended that students measure fuel mass changes – they carried out this experiment in Year 7. Tell students they have to look for all the 'ideal fuel' properties.

As a plenary to this activity, discuss reasons why 'butane' camping stoves are the most popular choice.

Answers: Q1, Q2 Students should use the 'ideal fuel' checklist on page 83 of the Student Book as a basis for discussing 'ideal' and 'non ideal' camping fuels.

■ *Activity 4* Answers: (a) CO_2, CO, SO_2, H_2O. CO is poisonous because it stops the blood carrying oxygen, SO_2 causes asthma and acid rain.
(b) (i) sulphur + oxygen → sulphur dioxide, $S + O_2 → SO_2$; (ii) hydrogen + oxygen → water, $2H_2 + O_2 → 2H_2O$.

Plenary and homework suggestions

■ *Review 5* can be carried out as a whole-class plenary on the board. Draw a cartoon fire and an aeroplane for the points to go underneath. The main teaching point is that fuel 'ideal' qualities vary with the use: (a) for a house a low maintenance fuel is important – no waste, pipelined supply, etc; (b) for an aeroplane, the fuel must be energy concentrated due to the difficulties of carrying large, heavy quantities.

■ 🖱 *Homework 6*. The 'Follow the mouse' box gives suggested websites. Students could write this up as an advert for CO detectors or as an article for the local paper etc.

Technician notes
Worksheet 32. What is the best fuel for camping stoves?
Demonstration

■ 'butane'-type camping stove (optional kettle or pan and tea-making things)
Goggles for each student

■ 'toffee' tray or small oven tray of sand
■ tin lids (small 'mince pie' metal dishes may work, but should be tested first to check they will not catch fire!)
■ heatproof mats, clamps and stands, boiling tubes, thermometer, stopclock, measuring cylinder, spills
■ access to wet cloths
■ fuels: firelighters (2 types), ethanol or paraffin burners (small amounts in crucibles), solid fuel tablets (from camping shops), wood shavings, newspaper

---

⚠ Safety

Goggles must be worn. Tell students how to extinguish fires. A full risk assessment must be carried out. Students with asthma or other breathing problems need to take extra care.

Unit 8 – Using chemistry

Energy from chemical reactions pp 84–85

Curriculum link

NC PoS: Sc3
Framework: P1, P5, SE4–SE6
QCA SoW: 9H Using Chemistry
Prior learning: 9E Reactions of Metals and Metal Compounds, 9F Patterns of Reactivity

Lesson guidance

Starter suggestions

- Revise the idea that chemical reactions involve energy changes. Demonstrate some reactions that give out energy, e.g. burning magnesium (tell students not to look directly at the flame), burning matches or an indoor firework or sparkler. Introduce the idea that chemical reactions can be useful energy sources, e.g. portable camping stoves (see last lesson), paraffin lamps, batteries, candles, magnesium flashbulbs etc.

Development

- *Energy changes in chemical reactions*. Revise ideas about *displacement reactions*. Ask students to look up 'displacement' in the glossary. Demonstrate the reaction between magnesium and copper sulphate and plate an iron nail using copper sulphate solution (see 'Displacement', page 26 in this book). For more able students, do word equations on the board. The reactions in Figure 1 can be shown to students (for the electrical energy demonstration, sulphuric acid gives a bigger 'flash').
- *Activity 1, Worksheet 33* Answers: Q1 (a) Magnesium/copper should give the largest change, iron/copper the smallest. (b) bigger. (c) No reaction, copper is less reactive than magnesium. Q2 Patterns should be similar. Demonstrate how to carry out the lemon experiment, and tell students to make sure they record voltages.
  Use a plenary discussion to elicit that a higher temperature change or voltage means that more energy is evolved. Discuss the advantages and disadvantages of using these reactions as energy sources, e.g. hazards, expense, environmental issues etc.
- *Activity 2* Answers: Potassium and gold. Potassium is too reactive/hazardous, gold is too expensive.
- *Activity 3* Answers: Examples – portable CD players (sound), toys (movement), games (light and sound) etc.
- *Using the energy*. Stress to students the advantages, but also the limitations, of using batteries.

- *Activity 4*. Discuss how the supply of metals is finite and that disposing of batteries in landfill sites causes toxic hazards. Ask students where rechargeable batteries are used, e.g. phones, cars etc.

Plenary and homework suggestions

- *Review 5*. As an extension, set up apparatus and draw it on the board, then ask students which systems would produce energy, e.g. silver in sodium chloride (No), two copper wires in a lemon (No) etc. Give several pairs of 'workable' metals and ask more able students to predict which system would produce the most energy.
- *Homework 6*. If any students know adults who work in car garages they could find out what happens to old car batteries. An Argos catalogue or similar has pricing information about batteries. Students should note that 'rechargeable' batteries can only be used for a set number of times.
- Students could carry out a web search into the disposal of batteries.

Technician notes
Demonstration of energy change reactions

- matches, tongs, magnesium ribbon, indoor sparkler or firework
- copper sulphate or sulphuric acid solution, $1 mol/dm^3$
- iron nail
- magnesium ribbon (small and long pieces)
- thermometer
- beaker, copper wire, 0.25 V bulb (and spares!) connected to leads and croc clips

Worksheet 33. Energy from chemical reactions

Goggles for each student
Temperature changes

- small pieces of magnesium ribbon, copper turnings, zinc, iron filings, copper sulphate, magnesium sulphate ($0.5 mol/dm^3$) boiling tubes, thermometers (0–50 °C if available)

Electrical energy

- petri dishes, voltmeters (to read less than 1 V), slices of lemon (orange works too)
- iron nails, copper wire, zinc foil or wire, 4 cm lengths magnesium ribbon
- sulphuric acid, $0.4 mol/dm^3$

Metals in batteries

- supply of old batteries

⚠ Safety

Goggles must be worn for student experiments and demonstrations. Acid splashes should be rinsed immediately. Copper sulphate solution is toxic.

Unit 8 – Using chemistry

The chemical industry

pp 86–87 ➤

Curriculum link

NC PoS: Sc1, Sc3
Framework: P1, SE1, SE5
QCA SoW: 9H Using Chemistry
Prior learning: 9E Reactions of Metals and Metal Compounds, 9F Patterns of Reactivity

Lesson guidance

Starter suggestions

■ Students may need help getting started. Lead them to think about (students will phrase these in their own words): research/inventing, testing new products, quality control, monitoring systems in industry, developing drugs, cosmetics, all categories of consumables. Develop the idea that chemists do not all wear white coats and work in labs.

Development

■ *What are chemicals used for?* Give students examples from each category, e.g. bulk chemicals includes iron and steel, and sulphuric acid which goes on to be used to make chemicals in the other four categories.

■ *Activity 1* is a fun activity with an important message. All packaging, most food, toothpaste, clothes, dyes, finishes on furniture, carpets etc. have been made using chemicals – every family buys £1300 worth of chemicals annually.

■ *Case study: Detergents.* In discussing this, tell students that people used to collect rain water for hair washing which had no dissolved rock in it, so that their hair did not end up full of scum. More expensive detergents are made from vegetable oils, e.g. palm oil and coconut oil. Stress how the development of improved products depended heavily on R&D by chemists.

■ *Activity 2, Worksheet 34.* Demonstrate the technique of each experiment. Show students what a lather looks like, and make sure they know what they are trying to time. Remind them that soap is more 'old fashioned' and was made from animal fat (usually whale blubber!).
Answers:
Q1 (a) You need a lot less detergent than soap to make a lather in hard water. Soap makes scum.
(b) Detergent – with soap, your hair would be full of scum; some people would prefer using non-animal products.
Q2 Adding soap flakes keeps the oil and water mixed longer but causes scum.
Q3 Detergent helps the oil mix with water so that it can be washed away.

■ *Activity 3* Answer: Soap removes oil more easily than just water, early detergents were unaffected by hard water, later detergents contain other performance enhancers and are biodegradable.

■ *Activity 4.* Look for information summarised at the end of Figure 2.

Plenary and homework suggestions

■ *Review 5.* This plenary can be run either as a class brainstorm, or each group could write a single point on a piece of paper to hold up to the rest of the class.

Differentiation/extension

■ Students can extend Activity 2, Worksheet 34 by trying to wash lipstick stains off scraps of cloth using pure water, cold water and soap or detergent, and hot water and detergent.

■ Many GCSE books contain diagrams showing how detergents emulsify oils: more able students could carry out further research to add detail to their activity answers.

Technician notes
Activity 1. Everyday things from chemicals

■ magazines showing consumables familiar to students
■ scissors, glue sticks, poster materials

Worksheet 34. How do soaps and detergents work?

■ hard water (make by shaking tap water with calcium carbonate, allow to settle and filter)
■ soft (or distilled) water
■ soap flakes on petri dishes, liquid detergent, test tubes with bungs, droppers
■ range of household detergents, e.g. bubble bath, washing up liquid, washing powder – can dispense in test-tube amounts, but allow students to see packages
■ vegetable oil, stopclock
■ (optional extension) small pieces of cloth with lipstick stains

---

⚠ **Safety**

This is a low-hazard activity, but check whether any student is allergic to the detergents used.

Unit 8 – Using chemistry

Mass and chemical change

pp 88–89 WS 35

Curriculum link

NC PoS: Sc1, Sc3
Framework: P1–P3, SE5
QCA SoW: 9H Using Chemistry
Prior learning: 9E Reactions of Metals and Metal Compounds, 9F Patterns of Reactivity

Lesson guidance

Starter suggestions

■ Students may be confused by the term 'mass'. Explain that it is possible to use a balance to measure mass before and after reactions have taken place. Ask students 'Where has the stuff gone?' for the match and the salty water examples. Introduce the idea that water/gases have entered the air.

Development

■ *The mass stays the same*. Show students some different coloured Lego® bricks. Stress that making different shapes from bricks makes no difference to the mass. Show with a balance that the mass of the new shape is always exactly the same as the starting mass of bricks. Link bricks with atoms rearranging themselves (see Student Book 2, page 52, 'Looking at Atoms'). Use bricks of two colours to model the iron sulphide reaction.

■ *Activity 1* Answer: 16 g.

■ *Reactions involving gases*. Students may not realise that gases have a mass – show this by weighing balloons before and after blowing up with different gases. A ruler 'see-saw' can be used with an empty balloon and a full one – the full one is heavier. Remind students about the basic equation format (reactants on left, etc).

■ *Activity 2*. See differentiation ideas below. Answers: wood + oxygen → carbon dioxide + water (+ ash), iron + oxygen → iron oxide. Wood gets lighter as gases go into the air. Iron gets heavier as it gains oxygen.

■ ▦ *Activity 3, Worksheet 35*. See extension below. Stress that students need to weigh everything (including containers) before and after, but that when a mass change is measured, weighing containers does not affect the result. Answers: Q1 The mass of the petri dish must be included in both weighings. Q2 The black copper oxide has gone, the solution goes blue. The mass stays the same because the same atoms are there – they have just rearranged themselves.

Q3 Candle gets lighter – gases are lost to the air (CO_2, H_2O). Copper gets heavier – oxygen gained.
Q4 Copper oxide; copper + oxygen → copper oxide.
Q5 (a) 3 g, (b) 7.5 g.
Q6 16 g; by making a number pattern from the table, e.g. 3:2 mass ratio.

Plenary and homework suggestions

■ Students must know the key indicators for chemical change: revisit those during this lesson. Ask, 'How can you tell a chemical change has happened?'

■ *Revision opportunities*. Ask students to use the glossary and their notes to revise key words: atom, element, compound, chemical change etc.

Differentiation/extension

■ *The mass stays the same*. More able students may suggest that the 'bricks' (atoms) may not be all the same mass. Fe atoms are heavier than S atoms, hence the mass of Fe is higher, though the atoms join in a 1:1 ratio.

■ *Activity 2*. Provide the reactant and product names for less able students to re-arrange into equations.

■ *Activity 3, Worksheet 35*. More able students can write word/formula equations for copper oxide and magnesium oxide reactions. Ask them to look at the table. Do they think magnesium or oxygen atoms are heavier?

Technician notes
Demonstrating mass staying the same
■ Lego® bricks of two colours
■ balloons (different gases, e.g. hydrogen, air), balance

Worksheet 35. Mass and chemical change
Goggles for each student
■ access to balance
■ petri dishes, beakers, spatulas, measuring cylinders
■ copper oxide; sulphuric acid, 0.4 mol/dm³
■ candles in holders or on petri dishes
■ copper turnings on tin lids
■ Bunsen, gauze, tripod, mat

⚠ Safety

Goggles must be worn. Any acid spills should be rinsed immediately. Warn students not to handle copper oxide until it is cool.

Unit 9 - Energy and electricity

Energy transfer and transformation

pp 90–91

Curriculum link

NC PoS: Sc4:5a,5b
Framework: E1, SE4
QCA SoW: 9I Energy and Electricity
Prior learning: 7I Energy Resources, 8I Heating and Cooling

Remind students: that energy is not a thing, substance, fluid or other tangible object; that different labels are used for different types of energy; and that one type of energy can be transformed into another. Students will need lots of practice to become familiar with the ideas of transfer and transformation.

Lesson guidance

Starter suggestions

■ Begin by asking students to list the energy types they have met before.

■ Use the cooling curves to talk about the transfer of thermal energy from the hot water to cooler molecules in the air. Discuss mechanisms of transporting energy, to help students deduce why a lid makes a difference. Many Sc1 skills may be practised during this activity.

Development

■ *What is energy?* The key idea here, that it is useful to keep track of energy, is developed further in the next lesson.

■ *Activity 1.* For the bungee jumper, groups use a small mass and springs in series. Give different groups different spring arrangements. Ask them to fix the clamp firmly to the bench, and to check that the falling mass does not tip the stand over. They must choose masses that do not permanently stretch the springs, and then adjust the drop height. Mention that, in a real bungee jump, it is painful and dangerous to have large decelerations.

■ *Activity 1 Answer:* To stretch a spring, we have to transfer energy to it. When you stretch a stiff spring and a loose spring by the same amount, the stiff spring stores more energy. Therefore, to store the same amount of energy in both springs, we have to extend the loose spring more than the stiff spring.

■ *'Differences cause change'* is a key idea. A hot body cools and a cooler environment warms up, and this happens naturally. A body in an environment at the same temperature will only become cooler if there is an energy

transformation. An energy difference needs to be harnessed to drive the cooling process in this instance. As another example, a stretched spring will contract naturally, and its potential energy can be harnessed to do tasks. To stretch the spring again, another energy transformation must be utilised.

■ *Activity 2, Worksheet 36.* Students analyse the collapse due to gravity of gas in a forming star using simple energy conservation ideas, and link this to Joule's measurement of a temperature difference between water at the top and bottom of a waterfall. Answers: Q1 GPE to KE to thermal energy. Q2 The particles have more KE on average. Q3 More mass means more gravity. Q4 More collapsing force due to gravity must be balanced by radiation pressure which increases as stars get hotter. So massive stars are hotter. Q5 Look back at Q1 answer; compare the basic processes involved.

Plenary and homework suggestions

■ *Review 3* Answer: The force of gravity between the book and the Earth is attractive. In separating the Earth and book, energy is transferred to the Earth/book system, analogous to stretching a toy spring in order to store energy.

■ *Review 4* Answer: As the bungee jumper falls, the gravitational PE of the Earth/jumper system decreases. We can account for the decrease in the increase in spring PE of the stretched bungee. Along the way, some of the initial gravitational PE will have been dissipated to thermal energy.

■ *Homework 5* Answer: light energy → chemical energy in chlorophyll to synthesise glucose from H_2O and CO_2

Differentiation/extension

■ ▣ Stress that, by identifying energy transformations, students can explain why something has happened. Extend faster students by giving them practice with this aspect of energy conservation quantitatively. Formulae they can use: change in GPE = mgh, KE = $\frac{1}{2}mv^2$, spring (Hooke's law) PE = $\frac{1}{2}kx^2$. k is known as the spring constant, and for any spring it is the gradient of its force–extension graph.

Technician notes
Activity 1. Bungee jumper
■ lab masses
■ several different springs
■ stand and clamp to fix it to bench

⚠ Safety

Instruct students to make sure their stand is firmly fixed. Warn them of the dangers of falling masses hitting toes and fingers.

Unit 9 – Energy and electricity

Energy accounting

pp 92–93

Curriculum link

NC PoS: Sc4:5c,5g
Framework: E1, SE4
QCA SoW: 9I Energy and Electricity
Prior learning: 7I Energy Resources, 8I Heating and Cooling

Lesson guidance

Starter suggestions

■ The idea of conserving energy means many things to many people, and the Starter elicits some of them. Use the table on *Worksheet 37* as a prompt. At this stage, discuss the ideas without too much detail, and steer students away from 'save the planet'-type issues.

Development

■ Keeping track of money, accounting, is a familiar idea to students. Energy is calculated in a similar way in physics, though energy is not a tangible 'thing'.

■ 🔍 *Activity 1*. The London Science Museum website is good:
http://www.sciencemuseum.org.uk Joule was an excellent investigator, and reflecting on how he did experiments is a good way for students to learn about Sc1. Ask them to write up their research on Joule: see the plenary suggestion for its use in a *PowerPoint* presentation or a poster.

■ *Activity 1* Answer: Joule's apparatus stirred the water as the weight fell: gravitational potential energy of weight → kinetic energy of paddle. He measured the increase in temperature of the water as frictional forces did work on the water. Joule found that the work done to lift the weight to the starting position and restore the weight's gravitational potential energy was proportional to the thermal energy gained by the water.

■ *Activity 2*. Each group collects data for analysis, applying the idea of conservation of energy: we must keep track of energy (accounting) in all its forms as it transfers and transforms. Carefully develop a class discussion of energy transformation from 'spring' potential energy to gravitational potential energy.

■ Groups can load the toys with plasticine and sketch graphs of jump height against total mass of toy using conservation arguments. Since we are assuming the initial spring PE to be constant, expect the jump height to be inversely proportional to the total mass. Most students will

appreciate that the spring stores a finite amount of energy. Some is dissipated and some transfers to gravitational potential energy of the Earth–toy 'gravity spring' system.

■ 🖩 🔍 Using a spreadsheet, data can be processed and graphs drawn clearly. Ensure that students use sensible scales. With the class, discuss the graphs, and error problems. This is an opportunity to develop Sc1 skills.

■ *Activity 3, Worksheet 37*. Ask students to work on their own. Then, when they have finished, they should discuss some sample answers in groups. Answers: Q1 KE in book dissipated to thermal energy in book and bench. Q2 KE in ball to GPE of ball and Earth; some dissipation due to air resistance forces. Q3 The molecules have their KE increased through collisions with moving piston; this energy is shared throughout the gas. The average KE of gas molecules increases. Q4 The motors have utilised electrical PE to increase GPE of the ride. Then GPE to KE and some dissipation. Q5 Radiation from the Sun transfers to electrical PE in panel, which can reverse chemical reactions in the cells, increasing chemical PE of cells again.

Plenary and homework suggestions

■ Invite groups to prepare short a *PowerPoint* presentation of their findings on the work of Joule in Activity 1, to show to the class in the next lesson. They can also produce a poster.

■ As a homework, ask students to turn their reports on Joule's work into a classroom poster.

Differentiation/extension

■ 🖩 *Activity 2*. The result that jump height decreases with load (in inverse proportion) can be developed for more able students:
jump height $\propto$ 1/total mass of toy.

■ 🖩 Ensure that all students understand the energy accounting idea. You can give faster students suitable formulae to make energy calculations. Formulae they can use: change in GPE = mgh, KE = $\frac{1}{2}mv^2$, spring (Hooke's law) PE = $\frac{1}{2}kx^2$. k is the spring constant, see page 36.

Technician notes
Activity 1. Joule's water paddle experiment
■ internet access to Science Museum website

Activity 2. Jumping toy
■ small spring-action jumping toy per group, available from most toyshops
■ ruler attached to clamp stand

Unit 9 – Energy and electricity

Electrical potential difference pp 94–95 → WS 38 WS 39

Curriculum link

NC PoS: Sc4:1c
Framework: E2, SE4
QCA SoW: 9I Energy and Electricity
Prior learning: 7I Energy Resources, 7J Electrical Circuits

Lesson guidance

Starter suggestions

- *Worksheet 38* can be completed in class discussion. Correct ideas: 1. Batteries transfer electrical PE to charges in circuits. When all their chemical PE is transformed to EPE they are dead. 2. Dynamos/generators and solar panels can drive current in a circuit. 3. The mobile charge in wires is urged to move when the battery is connected (charge moves in the battery also). Charge is never 'used up'. Energy, not charge, transformations take place in bulbs. 4. The mobile charges start moving almost everywhere simultaneously. Charge does not move around in a sequential motion from one component to the next. 5. How the charge flow divides depends on the resistance to flow of the branches: more flows through a branch of lower resistance.

- Show a *dry cell* cut open. Discuss the electrodes, electrolyte and chemical reactions in batteries. Elicit energy transfer explanations.

Development

- *Activity 1.* Check students' circuits. Expect them to measure about 1.8 V. Note: This fruit battery will *not* drive an LED or a bulb. It charges the capacitor, which then causes the LED to flash, like a camera flashgun. Develop the energy model for voltage: PDs (voltages) occur between points in the circuit where flowing charged particles (charges) transfer energy from EPE to other energy types. Link PD with charge separation.

- *Activity 2, Worksheet 39.* Students explore the idea of PD in a new context: display the capacitor in a flash camera. The capacitor should store sufficient energy at 1.8 V to make an LED flash briefly. Explain that defibrillators work similarly. Answers:
  Q1 Plus attracts minus charge; separating negative from positive charge requires an energy transfer to the charges.
  Q2. More positive and negative charge on each plate. The positive plate is positive because of an imbalance in the charge types.
  Q3. A decay curve, which is exponential.

Q4. No, the LED is not bright and it only flashes very briefly.

- *Activity 3.* For useful results, just a light source and voltmeter are required. Make sure the negative leg of the LED is clearly labelled for when students try to make it flash. They should carry out an energy analysis.

- Note: Diagrams containing electrons, as in Figure 2, page 95, and Figure 4, page 97, show their movement from negative to positive. For current flow in general (Figure 3, page 96), the flow is shown as the conventional positive to negative.

Plenary and homework suggestions

- *Review 4* Answer: Voltage is about energy transfer per unit charge. For a given amount of charge flow (current × time), the bigger the voltage across a device, the greater the energy transferred to it.

- *Review 5* Answer: In parallel, each bulb is connected separately across the full battery PD (voltage). In series, the voltage across each bulb *adds up* to the full battery PD.

- Students can try other fruit as cells. Is output voltage affected by the *depth* of the metal electrodes in the fruit, or their *spacing*.

- Students can explore the BP solar website **http://www.bpsolar.com/** and prepare a presentation on solar power for homework.

Differentiation/extension

- All students must be able to use the voltage addition rule for series circuits, and to explain why the full battery PD appears across a bulb connected in parallel. Faster students can be left to investigate the solar cell further.

Technician notes

Activity 1. Fruit battery
As Student Book page 95, Figure 1.
- lemon (squashed), tomato, 2 × Cu and 2 × Zn electrodes, connecting wires, crocodile clips, digital voltmeter and ammeter
- 2000 µF capacitor, LED

Worksheet 39. Flash!
Apparatus as for Activity 1, with capacitor, LED.
- flash camera taken apart to display capacitor

Activity 3. Portable power cell
As Student Book page 94, Figure 3.
- solar cell, 10 Ω resistor, ammeter, voltmeter, light source

---

⚠ Safety

Students *must not* touch the battery demonstration apparatus. They *must not* take disposable cameras apart themselves as very high voltages are produced.

Unit 9 – Energy and electricity

Electrical flow

pp 96–97 →

Curriculum link

NC PoS: Sc4:1a
Framework: E3, SE4
QCA SoW: 9I Energy and Electricity
Prior learning: 7I Energy Resources, 7J Electrical Circuits

Lesson guidance

Starter suggestions

■ 'Flow as speed' is the misconception most students bring with them from earlier stages, and 'flow as quantity of charge or water per second' is the key idea to establish before students tackle the Starter activity. With the class, discuss ideas of how to distinguish flow from speed, and write them on the board. In electrical circuits, quantity of charge flowing per second is electrical current. Answer: Students should suggest measuring water flow in cm^3 per second.

Development

■ *Water laws.* Help students to establish the idea that flow is conserved:
 – Total flow into a junction must equal total flow out along the branches.
 – The flow does not have to divide equally.
 – Water cannot go missing. (Ignore rain and evaporation here.)

■ *Activity 1.* With the class, review the correct ideas about current that they developed for Worksheet 38.

■ *Activity 2.* Students should work in groups as small as the equipment available will allow, so that all have hands-on experience. Set aside plenty of time for this activity. To avoid ammeters being inserted across batteries, get the students to build the circuit first, then to attach one wire only to the ammeter. To insert the ammeter, they must then break the circuit and use the ammeter and its wire to bridge the gap.
 📟 Students should write their experimental readings to an appropriate number of figures.

■ *Ammeter laws.* To compare with the water laws, gather results from the class and present them on the board.

■ *Activity 3.* To start the class thinking about an abstract and demanding physics model, refer back to Student Book 1, page 76, Diffusion and Gas Pressure. Use the idea of tiny invisible particles causing real pressure as a starting point for discussion of invisible charges in wires. If they need to revise the pressure idea, then develop it first, getting the students to summarise it in their own words.

Now ask students to imagine tiny charges in wires. The model of tiny, negative, moving charges in a wire can be used to summarise neatly all that students have observed in their circuit work. It is a powerful model. At this point, you can also discuss the general use of models in physics.

Plenary and homework suggestions

■ *Review 4* Answer: 0.2 A.
■ *Review 5* Answer: 0.6 A.
■ *Homework 6* Answer: It's the quantity of water flowing that's important. The river could be narrow and shallow.
■ As an alternative homework, ask students to review Worksheet 38 and write down which of their ideas about circuits has changed the most since they started this unit.

Differentiation/extension

■ Faster students will handle electron flow directly and will not need the water analogy.

Technician notes
Activity 2. Bulbs in series and parallel
■ 2 bulbs
■ suitable battery depending on bulb choice
■ ammeter
■ connecting wires

Unit 9 – Energy and electricity

Electricity in the home

pp 98–99 → WS 40

Curriculum link

NC PoS: Sc4:1c
Framework: E1, E3
QCA SoW: 9I Energy and Electricity
Prior learning: 7I Energy Resources, 7J Electrical Circuits

Lesson guidance

Starter suggestions

■ Answers: Boiling a kettle of water – EPE in wires → thermal energy in kettle element due to its resistance → thermal energy to water to boil it. Kettles used to make hot drinks at half time.

Development

■ *The mains.* 'The mains' supplies a large a.c. voltage. Domestic circuits look very unlike those in the lab, yet they are the same. Use Figure 1 or a simpler version to review series and parallel concepts. Introduce fuses, but not in detail.

■ *Activity 1.* The plugs that students wire up should have a nut and bolt screwed into all the pins so that they cannot be plugged into a socket. Explain 'live', 'neutral' and 'earth', and discuss the colour coding.

■ *Appliances transform electrical energy.* Discuss energy accounting ideas again, to reinforce the energy conservation principle.

■ *Watts.* Show the class some electricity bills and explain the details on them. List students' ideas on what they think we pay the electricity company for.

■ Display some domestic appliances with the power rating specification labels attached. Expand on the idea of power, which is difficult but will help students to utilise the data in Activity 2 and Worksheet 40. Relate the kWh to the joule.

■ *Activity 2* introduces some ideas about the relative energy efficiency of light sources.

■ *Activity 3, Worksheet 40.* You can lead this worksheet exercise as a class discussion, eliciting suitable findings from Activity 2. Answers: Q1 A = 61 lumens/watt; B = 15 lumens/watt; C = £12; D = £3.90; E = £9; F = £37.5; G = £21; H = £41.40. Q2 Fluorescent sources give more lumens per watt of electrical power. Q3 Incandescent bulb: EPE → light and heat energy in metal in bulb. Fluorescent bulb: EPE → UV light from mercury atoms → visible light from phosphor atoms; not much heat. Q4 The wire in the bulb is very thin compared to the cable wire. For a given current flow, thin wires get hotter – they have more resistance – than thick wires.

Plenary and homework suggestions

■ *Review 4.* Display and discuss the fuses and packaging details of the appliances they are suitable for. Answer: 13A fuse.

■ *Review 5.* Draw a large diagram on the board showing sockets and bulbs in parallel. The earth wire can be left out. Answer: If a socket or a bulb fails, current continues to flow through all the others.

■ Alternatives for *Homework 6.* Give students a simplified wiring diagram for two-way stair lighting and ask them to explain how the switching works.

■ Make a table showing power rating and fuse value for UK appliances, from which students can draw graphs or use mathematics to derive the relation between fuse value and power rating.

■ Ask students to revise the ideas of voltage, series and parallel in this unit.

Differentiation/extension

■ *Review 4.* Give more able students $P = V \times I$ to calculate the value of fuses. Others can have a table in a spreadsheet to guess the relation between power and fuse value for an appliance.

■ Faster students can learn about circuit breakers from the website **www.howstuffworks.com**

Technician notes

Activity 1. Wiring a plug
■ plug with pins blocked
■ fuse
■ small section of cable with ends of wires stripped
■ screwdriver

Electricity bills and appliances display
■ some electricity bills
■ domestic appliances with power rating labels

Activity 3, Worksheet 40. Fluorescent tubes versus incandescent light bulbs
■ internet access
■ optional for display: clear incandescent bulb and fluorescent tube

Review 4. Fuse display
■ fuses of different ratings and packaging
■ spreadsheet table of power ratings and fuse values for a range of appliances

Homework 6. Two-way switch
■ circuit diagram of two-way stair lighting

⚠ Safety

Warn students of the dangers of high voltages from the mains, and that they should *never* experiment with mains electricity.

Unit 9 – Energy and electricity

Generating power

pp 100–101

Curriculum link

NC PoS: Sc4:5c
Framework: E3, SE4, SE5
QCA SoW: 9I Energy and Electricity
Prior learning: 7I Energy Resources, 7J Electrical Circuits

Lesson guidance

Starter suggestions

- One nail and 50 turns of wire will make a strong electromagnet. Students measure the current flowing. Warn them that electromagnets get *hot*, and should not be left on. Let the students play with their electromagnet, just as Faraday did, to discover that relative motion between a coil and a permanent magnet can produce electrical power.
- The strong ceramic magnets available from equipment suppliers allow lots of simple experiments to be done very effectively.
- An LED can be made to flash by dropping a magnet through the coil. Two other gadgets that are fascinating at this stage are the self-powered radio and the shaking torch (see Worksheet 41).
- Again, employ the energy accounting idea to analyse energy transfers in complex machinery.

Development

- Show the students a bicycle *dynamo*. With a sensitive galvanometer, demonstrate how a voltage is induced in a dynamo by moving a wire relative to a magnet. Alternatively, use an electromagnet, switching it on and off near a coil connected to a sensitive galvanometer.
- *Activity 1.* With a large turned coil, simulate a shaking torch. Instruct groups to put a strong permanent magnet into a plastic measuring cylinder with a bung, and place the assembly inside the coil. Also, by shaking the magnet, students can charge a capacitor. The circuit is on Worksheet 41 but, for this Activity, omit the voltmeter.
- *Activity 2, Worksheet 41* provides a good summary to this section. Discuss the ideas students used in Activity 1 before they tackle the content of this worksheet. Answers: Q1 (a) Yes, according to our experiments, we get a bigger induced voltage the faster we move the magnet through the coil. (b) Yes, for a given rate of movement, the more coils we move the magnet through, the bigger the induced voltage.

- *Fuels and power stations.* Use energy transfer and transformation to analyse the use of fuels.
- *Activity 3, Worksheet 42.* The subject of wind power allows more depth for some students, and could also be adapted for homework. Answers: Q1 Use diagram of wind generator system. 100 J × efficiency of generator, etc. Q2 Thermal energy, 'heat', is generated. Q3 3.14 m². Q4 31.4 m³. Q5 Volume × density = 40.8 kg. Q6 2040 W. Q7 255 W.

Plenary and homework suggestions

- *Review 5.* Students' diagrams should show clearly the ideas demonstrated earlier.
- Ask students to find out how sea waves can be used to generate electricity.

Differentiation/extension

- *Review 5.* Faster students can suggest ways to make the voltage induction effect larger.
- Induced voltage is a difficult idea at KS3. It is sufficient if students can use a magnet and coil to drive an LED, but encourage those who want more detail and more investigation. Using energy analysis to work through energy transfers in a power station is a must for all students.

Technician notes
If apparatus for groups is limited, replace by a circus of several experiments.

Starter. A strong electromagnet
- iron nail, insulated wire coil
- switch, battery, connecting wires
- voltmeter and ammeter

Demonstrating how a dynamo works
- bicycle dynamo, connecting wires
- sensitive galvanometer to read at least 0.1 mA
- magnet – as strong as possible

Activity 1. Electromagnet and LED
- plastic measuring cylinder and bung
- strong magnet, e.g. ceramic cylindrical
- insulated copper wire coil with many turns wound on measuring cylinder
- LED, 2000 µF capacitor, connecting wires

Activity 2, Worksheet 41. Shaking dynamo
Components as for Activity 1, with:
- two or more insulated copper wire coils with different numbers of large turns
- voltmeter
- range of capacitors, 100–4000 µF

⚠ Safety

Warn students that electromagnets may get hot. Show students who use strong ceramic magnets the danger of trapping their fingers when the magnets are attracted to iron or other magnets.

Unit 10 - Gravity and space

Newton, the apple and the Moon

pp 102-103

WS 43

Curriculum link

NC PoS: Sc4:2b; Sc1:1a
Framework: F4
QCA SoW: 9J Gravity and Space
Prior learning: 7K Forces and their Effects; 7L The Solar System and Beyond

Lesson guidance

Starter suggestions

■ Demonstrate the whirly toy, asking students to watch carefully while thinking about orbits. The toy does not fly *out* and hit them. Discuss Newton's first law, and emphasise that the tension in the string is pulling the toy around its orbit. Group students so that they have space to experiment. Answers: As the mass of the load on the string increases, the rate of rotation has to increase. The toy is not moving towards the person's head. As you dive down a ride and then up for a loop you feel heavy; as you go over a bump you feel light.

Development

■ *How far is the Moon?* Most students appreciate that blocking out the Moon with a coin gives you some idea of its distance away. As Moon substitutes, make paper circles and paste them on the lab walls. The students find they need to hold a coin at a particular distance to just block out a circle.

■ 🖩 If suitable for your class, draw a diagram on the board of similar triangles showing eye position, and coin and Moon positions and diameters that allow the Moon's distance to be found.

■ 🖩 *Activity 1, Worksheet 43* Answers: Q1 The Sun's rays are parallel. With parallel lines, opposite angles are equal.
Q2 360°. Q3 36 × 500 = 18 000 miles.
The Greeks studied lunar eclipses and estimated how many Moon diameters fitted into the Earth's shadow at eclipse.

■ 📖 *The universal law of gravity.* Copy some of the pages of *Principia* from:
(http://www.fordham.edu/halsall/mod/new ton-princ.html)
Most students find Newton's language amusing and strangely captivating! Convey that this great scientist used experimental evidence and other information to create a law to describe *what* was happening. He created the mathematics needed to represent the law of gravity, and then started to worry about *how* gravity worked. Newton was

using laws derived on Earth to describe what was happening throughout the universe. Modern physics was born.

■ *Activity 2.* Students are always keen to talk about rollercoasters. It's the accelerations – 'g' units – that make these rides exciting. The accelerations make your weight change as you go over or down into a loop. For Activity 2 in the next lesson, explain that g = 10 N/kg on Earth. Everyone has seen weightless astronauts on TV. Jumping, we all feel weightless when falling freely in gravity. When the floor stops us, we feel weight.

Plenary and homework suggestions

■ *Review 3.* Figure 2 and its text touch on the inverse square idea, but it need not be quantitative. Of importance is the idea of gravity getting weaker as we move away from Earth. Stress that gravity is not associated with the atmosphere – gravity operates on the Moon which has no atmosphere. The force is towards the centre of the Earth, or any other body. 'Down' only has meaning when we know the direction of the gravitational force. Answer: A ninth of the attraction at Earth's surface.

■ *Review 4* Answer: Twice the attraction.

■ 🖱 *Homework 5.* As an alternative, lots of websites exist for a project comparing rollercoaster accelerations.

Differentiation/extension

■ Give less able students help with Worksheet 43. Those with good maths skills may complete it with little difficulty, and grasp the inverse square law.

Technician notes
Starter. Rotating toy
See the Starter diagram on page 102.
■ 1.5 m string
■ 20 cm plastic tube
■ 5 weights, each 20 to 50 g
■ rubber bung

How far is the Moon?
■ 4–5 cm diameter paper circles
■ coins

⚠ Safety

Warn students to take care when operating the rotating toy.

Unit 10 – Gravity and space

Weight and mass

pp 104–105 ⟹

Curriculum link

NC PoS: Sc4:2b,4a–c; Sc1:1a
Framework: F4, SE1
QCA SoW: 9J Gravity and Space
Prior learning: 7K Forces and their Effects; 7L The Solar System and Beyond

Lesson guidance

Starter suggestions

- Answers: Aristotle supported the concentric spinning spheres model. He thought this right and natural because the sphere is the perfect shape. Thus the Sun, Earth, Moon and stars must also be spheres. The heavens are composed of perfect regions of unchangeable order, with bodies moving in perfect circular orbits. All this is in stark contrast to our modern models.
- Ask the class: What is mass? What is weight? Summarise the students' answers on the board. And note the main misconceptions to be dealt with during the lesson.
- Give students research time or set a homework to research one early Solar System model. Remind the class of the meaning of the term 'model'.

Development

- *Ancient models have changed.* The opportunity to present a nice story about how science has developed and works is too good to miss in this lesson. The cyclic activity of experimental evidence, stimulating thought and model making, then more experiment, is the central theme of scientific investigation. Here you can present and explore the history of ideas about the Solar System as an example of the scientific method.
- *Activity 1, Worksheet 44.* Organise students in pairs. They watch the accelerating masses and the balance readings. If done carefully with many repeats, they will see the balance readings change. This links nicely to the previous lesson's study of weightlessness. Ensure that students let the string slip through their fingers and not just drop the mass and balance. Warn about toes and fingers getting squashed.
  For Einstein's ideas, these are good sites:
  http://virtualastronaut.jsc.nasa.gov/lessons /fallintoMathematics.pdf
  http://spacelink.nasa.gov/Instructional. Materials/NASA.Educational.Products/ Microgravity/
- *Activity 2.* Direct students to sources of the masses of the Moon, Jupiter and Mars, or give them data on the number of times greater the

masses of these bodies are than Earth. See:
http://seds.lpl.arizona.edu/nineplanets/nine planets/nineplanets.html
- *Gravity maps.* If available, show from the Nick Park video 'Wallace and Gromitt, Grand Day Out', the snippet where Wallace on the Moon kicks the ball up and it does not come down! This makes a great discussion point.
- *Making a gravity map.* It is common in physics to make a picture like Figure 1 on page 104 to illustrate an equation. The arrows here represent the gravity field.
- If students are able, they can use *Excel* to do more work on calculating inverse squares.

Plenary and homework suggestions

- *Review 3.* Emphasise mass as amount of stuff, measured in kg, and weight as a force, measured in newtons.
- *Review 4.* Students can prepare a *PowerPoint* presentation of their findings for the fall of a hammer and feather experiment after watching the video referenced in 'Follow the mouse'. You can set this activity as a nice homework.

Differentiation/extension

- For mathematically inclined students, this lesson can be made quantitative. Encourage students with less maths ability to describe the law of gravity qualitatively. The force of attraction on 1 kg placed near a planet depends on the mass of the planet and the separation between the 1 kg mass and the centre of the planet. The separation factor is an inverse square, which will need careful discussion. Using brightness, which decreases as an inverse square may offer a way to discuss this concept.

Technician notes
Activity 1, Worksheet 44. Gravity disappears
See the assembled apparatus on the worksheet.
- pulley or round bar
- 3 m strong string
- spring balance
- weights of 5–100 g

Activity 2. Weight on the Moon, Jupiter and Mars
- internet access; books containing data: see references above
- Nick Park video: Wallace and Gromit, Grand Day Out, see **http://www.aardman.com/**

⚠ Safety

Warn the class about damage to limbs by falling masses. Tell the students to pull on the string or let it slip through their fingers. They should not let it go.

Unit 10 – Gravity and space

Planets and satellites

pp 106–107 ➡

WS 45

Curriculum link

NC PoS: Sc4:2b; Sc1:1a
Framework: F4
QCA SoW: 9J Gravity and Space
Prior learning: 7K Forces and their Effects; 7L The Solar System and Beyond

Lesson guidance

Starter suggestions

■ This lesson builds on the Newton and Apple story. Discussion of rollercoasters will lead the class into the work. The students must understand that gravity controls orbital motion of all satellites, not just the Moon.

■ Looking at rollercoaster websites can be useful, but you will need to select suitable portions to use.

Development

■ *Acceleration at constant speed.* 'Acceleration means speeding up,' is what most students will be thinking. Here, they also need to appreciate that change of motion could involve constant speed, in terms of distance/time, but direction change. This is important if orbital motion is to be understood. You could demonstrate again the whirly toys from the lesson 'Newton, the Apple and the Moon'.

■ *Newton and orbits.* Newton's famous cannon picture is the main talking point for this section. It leads on nicely to talking about orbits. The key idea here is: Accelerations do not always produce speed changes.

■ *Activity 2.* It is interesting to reflect on the fact that the rotation of our planet can help a rocket to reach the right orbit speed when launched in the direction of the Earth's rotation, and at the Equator. Many launch sites are close to the Equator. This activity will produce research material for discussion or for students to prepare a report on this effect.

■ *Activity 3, Worksheet 45* Answers: Q1 As you move from the centre of the ride, your rotational speed increases in proportion to your distance from the centre. Q2 At the North Pole, speed is zero (as at the roundabout centre), at the Equator, the speed is at a maximum on Earth (as right at the edge of the roundabout). It then gets smaller as you walk from the Equator to the South Pole. Q3 At the Equator. Q4 There are lots of sites close to the Equator.

Plenary and homework suggestions

■ Explain how Newton's cannon and hill picture helps us to understand orbital motion.

Differentiation/extension

■ Faster students can follow a more quantitative route through the material.

■ *Activity 1.* For more able students, you can present data to explore Kepler's third law which gives the relationship between the dimensions of planetary orbits and the time it takes to travel them. He found that distance^3/time^2 is a constant. By distance we mean orbital radius (approximately), and time is orbital period. This relationship is shown in the following data for the moons of Jupiter which Kepler published in 1619, and which later helped Newton to formulate his law of gravity.

Name	Distance from Jupiter (miles)	Time of orbit (hours)	Distance^3/time^2 A constant!
Io	262 220	42.36	1.005×10^{13}
Europa	417 190	85.23	9.996×10^{12}
Ganymede	665 490	171.71	9.996×10^{12}
Callisto	1 170 700	400.54	1.000×10^{13}

■ 🖩 You can ask students to confirm the values in the last column, and to show just how clever Kepler was to work out this law.

Unit 11 – Speeding up

Speed

pp 108–109

Curriculum link

NC PoS: Sc4:2a
Framework: F1, SE6
QCA SoW: 9K Speeding up
Prior learning: 7K Forces and their Effects

Lesson guidance

Starter suggestions

■ Students should appreciate that to calculate speed they need to measure the time interval and the distance covered. Tackle the misconception that heavy masses make the trolley roll down the slope faster. There is useful data in.
http://www.caranddriver.com

Development

■ *Measuring speed*. Emphasise that measuring time and distance will involve error. Discuss techniques and devices used to measure speed, including the car speedometer and motion sensor (used in Activity 1), light gates and ticker tape.

■ *Activity 1, Worksheet 46*. To review sound waves and echo location, refer to Student Book 2, pages 118 and 127. Suggest students think of a pulse of sound as an 'object' moving like a ball through the air. The pulse has a measurable time of leaving its source and a time of arrival at another point. In this exercise, students find out how echo location works in theory but, if convenient, you can demonstrate the equipment.
Answers: Q1 1/330 s or 3.03 ms. Q2 1/165 s or 6.06 ms. Q3 333 m/s.

■ *Activity 2*. Discuss the car speedometer (Figure 1). Give the data in the table on the right for the Porsche and Volvo V70 and ask students to draw graphs using a spreadsheet. Then discuss what the data is showing them and what they expected to see. Answers: The graphs are very similar but show that the Porsche has greater acceleration.

■ *Athletic's race 1*. Show a table of 100 m world record times. Ask the students to examine the figures and to comment on the difficulty of setting a new world 100 m record.

■ *Activity 3*. Give pairs of students a metre ruler and stopwatch and ask them to work out how to measure reaction time. (They may have already done this for Worksheet 9.) Help those who have no idea. You need not introduce $g = 9.8$ m/s², but instead circulate a data table that converts ruler length to time. A reaction time of 0.1 seconds is phenomenal.

Plenary and homework suggestions

■ Students can work out average speeds for their journey to school, and the speed of the Earth round the Sun (average distance from Earth is 150 million km). They need to say why the speeds are averages.

Differentiation/extension

■ *Activity 2*. More advanced students can examine the slopes of the graphs they draw. Then talk about acceleration.

■ To develop their numeracy skills, give faster students the data in the Porsche/Volvo table without the m/s column. Ask them to convert the mph data to m/s by setting up the correct formula in the m/s column in the spreadsheet, then to think about their answers: Are they getting sensible speeds for cars?

■ *Activity 3*. Reaction time is calculated from the formula, drop length = $\frac{1}{2} \times g \times t^2$. More able students will enjoy seeing where the formula comes from.

Technician notes
Starter: Trolley on a slope
Demonstration and optionally a group activity
■ dynamics trolley, slope, lab masses
■ timer/motion sensor

Worksheet 46. Bat sensor demonstration
■ dynamics cart
■ computer (connected to motion sensor)
■ program software for chosen sensor
■ motion sensor
■ light gate if not seen by students before
■ stopwatch or clock

Athletics race 1
■ displayed or photocopied list of 100 m world record times over the last 30 years

Measuring reaction time
■ stopwatch and metre ruler
■ table converting length of ruler drop to time

Speed in mph	Speed in m/s	Time (s) it takes to reach speed	
		Volvo	**Porsche**
0	0	0	0
30	13	2.7	1.8
40	18	4.0	2.9
50	22	5.4	3.9
60	27	7.2	5.2
70	31	9.4	6.8
80	36	11.8	8.8
90	40	14.5	10.9
100	44	18.8	13.6
110	49	–	16.7
120	53	29.9	
130	58	38.1	

Unit 11 – Speeding up

Changing speed

pp 110–111 →   WS 47

Curriculum link

NC PoS: Sc4:2c
Framework: F1, SE4
QCA SoW: 9K Speeding up
Prior learning: 7K Forces and their Effects

Lesson guidance

Starter suggestions

- Discuss acceleration, emphasising the idea of *change* in speed.
- 🖩 🖱 Produce some changing speed data using a motion sensor, ticker tape etc. Download film of a water rocket from:
  http://ast.leeds.ac.uk/~knapp/rockets/
  and ask the students to produce graphs and discuss the graph shapes.

Development

- *Unbalanced forces produce changes in motion*. Concentrate on unbalanced forces producing *accelerations* – speeding up and slowing down. Balanced forces result in no *change* in motion, but maintain constant speed (*not* just standing still). Counter the misconception that you need an unbalanced driving force to sustain motion. Initially, forces must be unbalanced to accelerate an object. In the absence of friction, motion will continue unchanged if the initial force is then removed.
- *Activity 1*. If used as a practical, each student needs a block of wood, about 0.5 kg mass and an attached spring balance. Otherwise describe Figure 1 as showing two blocks on a bench and ask students to identify what interaction might be the cause of each of the forces. When a block is moving at constant speed, the reading on a spring balance attached to it is relatively stable. The spring pull on the block can balance the friction force between the block and bench. Accelerate the block and you can see the spring balance reading increase suddenly. Answers: In adding force, direction must be taken into account. 5 N plus 5 N can equal 0 N!
- 🖩 *Activity 2*, on unbalanced force resulting in change of motion (change in speed per second), can be made quantitative for faster groups. Allow the masses, connected to the trolley, to hang over the edge using a pulley. The weight of trolley and mass provides a force to accelerate the trolley. A box to catch falling weights is useful.
- *Activity 2* Conclusion: A larger unbalanced force produces a larger speed change. For a given falling mass, the total mass being accelerated controls the speed change over a given distance.

- *Activity 3*. The data is for the 1996 Summer Olympics, Donovan Bailey in the 100 metres and Michael Johnson in the 200 metres.

Bailey		Johnson	
Time (s)	Position (m)	Time (s)	Position (m)
0	0	0	0
1.9	10	6.3	50
3.1	20	10.12	100
4.1	30	11.4	112.9
4.9	40	14.0	140.3
5.6	50	14.8	149.4
6.5	60	16.2	167.7
7.2	70	17.0	176.9
8.1	80	17.8	186
9.0	90	19.32	200
9.84	100		

- Students draw position–time graphs and discuss their shapes. Show them how to make rough speed–time graphs using a spreadsheet. This leads to the two-phase sprint model. Average speeds may provoke a discussion of who was the better athlete.
- *Activity 4, Worksheet 47* gets students looking at total braking distance against speed data. Stress that to change the speed of a car to zero requires a steeply increasing braking distance as speed increases, not a proportional increase. Answer: Q1 4 m.

Plenary and homework suggestions

- Ask students to produce speed–time graphs for their journey to school by car, then collect and compare it.
- Students can create a concept map for this lesson, adding suitable diagrams to illustrate the concepts recorded.

Differentiation/extension

- All students must know how to add forces in simple situations to get a total force. They must understand that an unbalanced condition causes motion change. Faster students may measure accelerations and work with slopes of speed–time graphs.

Technician notes

Activity 1. Forces on a block
- wood block, 0.5 kg mass, spring balance

Activity 2. Trolley and different falling masses
- stopwatch
- dynamics trolleys
- pulley arrangement to connect a falling mass to the trolley
- box to catch falling weights

Worksheet 47. Braking distances
- internet access for Highway Code data
- computer with *Excel*

Unit 11 – Speeding up

Bubbles and parachutes

pp 112–113 ➔

Curriculum link

NC PoS: Sc4:2d
Framework: F1
QCA SoW: 9K Speeding up
Prior learning: 7G Particle Model of Solids, Liquids and Gases, 7K Forces and their Effects

Concentrate on the idea of adding forces to get a balanced force condition. Revise relevant ideas from Year 7. Avert the notion that force makes movement, and that if there is no force forward then there is no movement forward. Emphasise that unbalanced forces produce changes in motion. Some will find difficulty at first with forces that depend on factors such as cross-sectional area and speed.

The other issue is the essential difference between speed and velocity. Some groups need more time to grasp this than others: students will naturally talk about 'speed' most of the time but always a 'terminal velocity', which they think about as a special speed.

Lesson guidance

Starter suggestions

- Show photos of Olympic swimmers, cyclists or downhill skiers. Ask: Why do they wear their special clothing? Summarise ideas on the board. Draw out the idea of reducing drag force.
- Ensure that the students realise that the weight of the paper has not changed, but that the fall times change dramatically. Relate this idea to the issues described above.

Development

- *Feeling friction.* Moving objects push molecules out of the way, and the molecules resist. The factors that affect the size of the resistance are many. The students need to grasp the idea that cross-sectional area and speed are key factors. For the dragged block, its weight is important.
- *Activity 1* gives students an intuitive feel for what we mean by the terms friction force and drag. Students should conclude that cross-sectional area and speed of movement affect drag.
- *Activity 3, Worksheet 48.* Rising bubbles are used to explore the interplay between drag and liquid upthrust. Before students start, as a demonstration, make some air bubbles in glycerol and project images on a screen or, better, allow the students to make bubbles in small groups. See the arrangement in the photos of Worksheet 48:
  – Air bubbles are introduced into a small tank of glycerol using a glass pipette connected by

tubing to a small syringe.
  – A grid or ruler is used to measure the size and ascent speed of the bubbles.
  – Use an OHP to project fizzy water bubbles, and contrast their motion with that of bubbles in glycerol.

- *Worksheet 48* Answers: Q1 Distance moved/time taken shows that the big bubble moves faster. The fact that the speed does not change between consecutive pairs of photos indicates that terminal velocity has been reached. Q2 The bigger bubbles, having a larger volume, have a larger upthrust force acting on them. The drag force on them depends on their radius and speed. For terminal velocity, the upthrust and drag must be balanced. The bigger bubbles must be moving faster when upthrust and drag balance.
- *Terminal velocity* is developed through discussing sky diving. The key idea here is of a variable drag force (varying with speed and area) eventually balancing weight or upthrust.
- *Activity 4, Worksheet 49.* Measurements show terminal velocity for a falling coffee filter. Answers: Again, the speeds show that terminal velocity is reached. This could be extended into an investigation: stacking filters can change weight and terminal velocity.

Plenary and homework suggestions

- 🖩 Drawing a speed–time graph for a skydiver is an important exercise.

Differentiation/extension

- All students must be able to explain why a skydiver or cat can reach a terminal velocity, using the concept of balanced forces. To do this they must appreciate how drag forces can vary with shape and speed of an object. Ask more able students to work out distance travelled from speed–time graphs.

Technician notes
Worksheet 48. Bubbles demonstration
- small tank, e.g. rectangular vase
- glycerol
- syringe connected by tubing to a pipette
- ruler or grid to measure size and distance bubbles travel
- stopwatch

⚠ Safety

Glycerol is a sticky substance, and students should be warned to avoid contact with it.

Unit 12 – Pressure and moments

What is pressure?

pp 114–115 >

Curriculum link

NC PoS: Sc4:2g; Sc1:2k
Framework: F3, SE4
QCA SoW: 9L Pressure and Moments
Prior learning: 7K Forces and their Effects

Lesson guidance

Starter suggestions

■ Pressure as force/area is one objective, and this is quite easy to teach. To revise gas pressure as a dynamic bombardment, which some students find a difficult concept, see 'Diffusion and Gas Pressure' from Year 7 (Student Book 1, page 76). Start by asking what atmospheric pressure means. How could the pressure of gas from the gas supply be measured? You can demonstrate a measurement of this using a manometer.

■ The students can compress a gas and measure a change in water level on a simple glass U-tube manometer. No explanations are required at this stage.

Development

■ *Pressure is force ÷ area*. A bed of nails is not dangerous but students find this difficult to believe. A discussion of the bed of nails will lead naturally on to pressure as force/area. Discuss with the class the usual examples of skis, skates, drawing pins etc.

■ *Bombardment*. We can think about atmospheric pressure as weight/area. It is more useful for later work to think about gas pressure as due to molecular bombardment.

■ *Activity 1*. Though you can demonstrate this, it is more instructive for students to do it themselves. The idea that force on the balance can be produced by lots of little collisions surprises some students. The marble weighs the same as all the ball bearings.

■ ◎ *Activity 2*. The fact that the little balls do not hit simultaneously, and that they are spread out over a large area, was used to design low mass protective shields for spacecraft.

■ ◎ *Activity 2* will allow you to do some research training using websites.

■ *Cartesian diver demonstration*. Buoyancy is a nice pressure effect to discuss, and Galileo's thermometer is an unusual context. At this stage, you can demonstrate the Cartesian diver experiment. Use a drinks bottle and a sachet of ketchup (mayonnaise doesn't work as well!). Insert the sachet, fill the bottle with water and screw on the top. Squeezing the bottle causes the air in the sachet to be compressed, reducing the upthrust force on it, and the sachet sinks. Releasing the bottle allows the sachet to return to the surface. Students can see this effect clearly when a short length of a plastic straw sealed with plasticine is used: the straw visibly collapses when the air is squashed.

■ *Activity 3*. Students witness the ball responding to a buoyancy force. They have to load the ball so that it just rises to the surface, balancing forces (although not perfectly).

Plenary and homework suggestions

■ Give some simple calculations involving the use of the equation pressure = force/area. Also set work where students have to use the idea of pressure to explain a phenomenon, such as the Cartesian diver.

Technician notes

Starter. Atmospheric pressure
■ plastic syringe, tubing and glass U-tube
■ manometer attached to gas supply

Activity 1. Dropping masses
■ marble (or large ball bearing)
■ small ball bearings, total mass = marble's mass
■ kitchen scales or balance

Cartesian diver demonstration
■ 2 litre drinks bottle of water with screw top
■ sachet of ketchup
■ 1–3 cm lengths of a plastic straw
■ plasticine

Activity 3. Sinking a ping-pong ball
■ ping-pong ball
■ large beaker
■ tape, string and nuts

Unit 12 – Pressure and moments

Using the idea of pressure

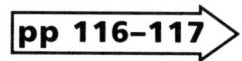 pp 116–117 WS 50

Curriculum link

NC PoS: Sc4:2g
Framework: F3
QCA SoW: 9L Pressure and Moments
Prior learning: 7K Forces and their Effects

Lesson guidance

Starter suggestions

- Pneumatics and hydraulics use the idea of pressure in gases and liquids. Give the students a plastic syringe and a beaker of water. Explain to groups that gases can be squashed. Tell them to block the end of a syringe with air inside, and push in the plunger. The gas changes volume. Then tell them to fill the syringe with water and repeat. The difference in behaviour is striking. It takes practice to fill the syringes with water and omit air bubbles. If bubbles get in, you can introduce the dangers of air in hydraulic braking systems. Discussion of car braking systems, particularly the high brake pad pressure needed to slow down the vehicle, is useful.

Development

- *Activity 1* uses hydraulic pressure to lift a load with the apparatus shown below, set up either as a demonstration or by students.

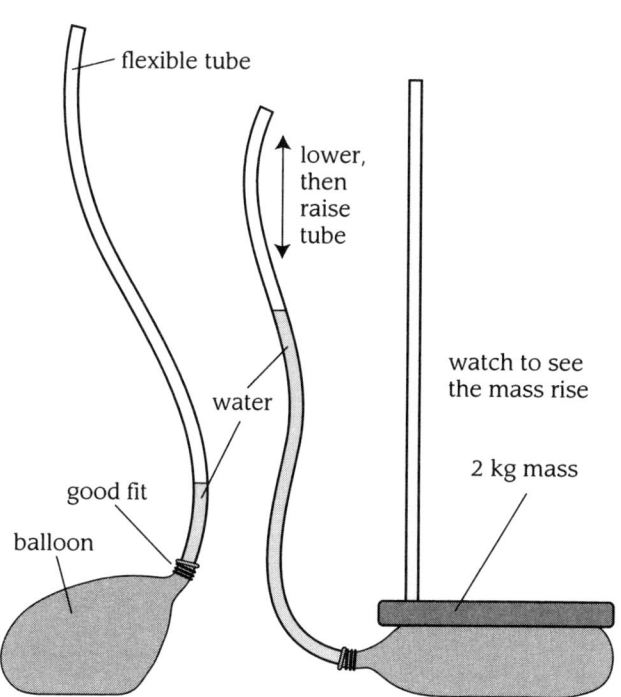

flexible tube

lower, then raise tube

water

watch to see the mass rise

2 kg mass

good fit

balloon

Use the particle model to discuss the fact that gases are compressible but liquids are practically incompressible.

- *Activity 2* should be fun and can be made quantitative. You can feel a difference when the large piston is connected to the retort stand and the small piston is the drive piston. The force differences can be measured roughly using a kitchen balance. Also, the lever arm length can be changed and its effect measured with kitchen balance. For some students, you can introduce the idea of a moment.

- *Scuba diving* is a great context for summarising all the work on pressure. Buoyancy, increased liquid pressure with depth, and physics of gas pressure are all relevant to diving and must be understood by divers.

- 🖰 *Activity 3* is a simple exercise, requiring students to use the website reference and then to calculate the total pressure at a given depth. This could be pen and paper also.

- *Boyle's law* is KS4 but can be mentioned and usefully discussed at KS3. It need not be quantitative and, with data logging, graphs illustrating the law can be generated easily.

- *Activity 5, Worksheet 50* takes the students through a practical calculation of a very important number. It's a matter of life and death and must be understood by all divers. Answers: Q1 2000/28 = 71.43 minutes. Q2 4 times atmospheric, 10m down increases local pressure by atmospheric. Q3 4 times the pressure means the tank will last only a quarter of 71.43 minutes!

Plenary and homework suggestions

- 🖰 There are many websites on the physics of scuba. The 'How stuff works' site is good on hydraulic machines. The students can prepare a slide or *PowerPoint* presentation on scuba or hydraulics.

Differentiation/extension

- 🖩 For faster students, Boyle's law can be made quantitative, and proportion can be worked on using the gas laws.

Technician notes

Starter. Applying pressure to air and water
- 10 cm³ and 20 cm³ syringes
- length of tubing

Activity 1. Hydraulics to raise a load
- 1 m of flexible tube
- balloon that fits securely to tube
- 2 kg lab weight

Activity 2. Hydraulics and pneumatics
- 10 cm³ and 20 cm³ syringes
- flexible tubing and balloon
- clamp stand

Unit 12 – Pressure and moments

Levers

pp 118–119

WS
51

Curriculum link

NC PoS: Sc4:2e,2f
Framework: F2, SE4, SE6
QCA SoW: 9L Pressure and Moments
Prior learning: 7K Forces and their Effects

Lesson guidance

Starter suggestions

■ Levers enable us to do jobs more easily – they reduce the effort we have to use to lift or move something. They do not save us energy: most of the time, they allow us to use smaller forces to do a job. But sometimes speed of movement is the desired outcome. For example, considering hand movement, the skeletal lever system has been designed to optimise hand speed (see Activity 2). Start by talking about how a ramp might be used to lift a piano.

■ Opening a door that is leant on allows students to feel the effect of using a lever to move a load.

Development

■ *Simple machines.* Develop the piano ramp example, being careful to show that the ramp does not save energy.

■ *Activity 1, Worksheet 51* gives students hands-on experience of a balanced see-saw before they convert it to use as a lever.
Answers: Q1 The statement is a little vague, but essentially conveys the idea. It is better to talk about distances of loads and effort from pivot points, see Q2.
Q2 Small mass × big distance to pivot point = large load × its distance to pivot point. Don't worry too much about mass being used instead of force or weight. However, some groups will work with force from the outset. When students have finished, guide them to the 'law of the lever', that small forces moving a large distance can move big masses a smaller distance.

■ *Activity 2.* A model arm is used to demonstrate levers in the body. The lever that is the lower arm and biceps muscles is not designed to minimise moving force. The hand moves quickly for small changes in muscle length and this is useful. The activity explores the biceps insertion point on the lower arm, and hand movement, and it can be extended to show the role of the triceps muscle, which joins the elbow to the shoulder.

■ Show that the bottle opener and wheelbarrow are really the same machine.

■ *Activity 3.* All students will put card close to the scissors hinge to cut. Get them to analyse this behaviour using the lever analysis. The position of the effort from fingers is fixed. Putting the load/resistance close to the hinge/pivot will allow minimum effort to be used to cut the card. At the same time, the cutting process takes longer, and the effort moves through a bigger distance.

■ *Trebuchet.* The trebuchet was a truly remarkable machine. A model can be seen working on the 'Follow the mouse' website. Its lever structure in Figure 4 is apparent. Large amounts of energy were transferred to massive projectiles using a very massive counterbalance. The long throwing arm moves very fast.

Plenary and homework suggestions

■ *Activity 3* can be set for homework.

■ Ask students to list all the levers that they see at home, then to analyse the levers, saying whether they allow smaller forces moving through bigger distances to do jobs.

Technician notes
Worksheet 51. The law of the lever
■ 30 cm ruler
■ pencil
■ nuts, washers or coins

Activity 2. A model arm
■ 2 lolly sticks with holes made as in Figure 2
■ means of attachment for sticks
■ string

Activity 3. Cutting card
■ paper; thick card
■ scissors

⚠ Safety

Warn students to take care using scissors and never to hand them over point first.

Unit 12 – Pressure and moments

Moments and stability

pp 120–121

Curriculum link

NC PoS: Sc4:2f; Sc1:2k,2m
Framework: F2
QCA SoW: 9L Pressure and Moments
Prior learning: 7K Forces and their Effects

Lesson guidance

Starter suggestions

- You can begin the lesson by looking at photos of vehicles with high and low centres of gravity. Students will know intuitively which is more stable. The question is: Why? Centre of mass need not be discussed at this stage.
- The Starter activity gets the students making a balancing toy that looks improbable. This is fun and really engages the class. Allow groups plenty of time to get their toys balancing.

Development

- *Moments.* A see-saw apparatus can be given to pairs of students. With little help they will learn to balance a large load with a small load by positioning the masses appropriately. To start with, they should balance the ruler in the middle, to avoid dealing with the unseen weight of the balancing beam.
- 🖩 *Activity 1.* Guide the groups very carefully so that all students are able to calculate moments and develop their algebra skills.
- The microbalance (Figure 2) makes a beautiful investigation for faster students. They can try to find the mass of hair. They will need help to set up a scale for the balance.
- *Balance.* Discuss the crane photo and run through the text. Balancing moments to account for stability is the key idea here.
- *Activity 3.* Set up the balanced structures shown in Figure 4 on page 120, and lead the class through the activity. Half the class could work on the first structure, while the rest work on the second, two-spring-balance structure. Ask them to identify clockwise and anticlockwise moments. Warn students that in the one-spring-balance structure, the ruler can flip up, tipping masses on to the floor.
- *Activity 4.* The Lego® tower experiment will allow you to bring in qualitatively the idea of centre of mass. If used in the Starter, the vehicle photos can be discussed again in the light of this activity.
- Judo is a sport where moments and stability – careful control of own and opponent's centre of mass – are the keys to success. You can induce potential instability in your opponent by forcing their centre of mass upwards. The idea of a high centre of mass is also crucial to understanding why sports utility vehicles (SUVs) are so unstable and why rollover is a major current issue.

Plenary and homework suggestions

- A good homework here is to write up the Lego® tower investigation. It allows students to elaborate on stability in relation to centre of mass. The errors are large and need careful discussion in this experiment.

Differentiation/extension

- Calculations using the weight of the beam to balance a load could be discussed with faster students.

Technician notes

Starter. Balancing toy
- stiff wire and 2 nuts
- piece of dowel
- vehicle photos (optional)

Moments and a microbalance
- ruler, pivot
- U-shaped support as Figure 2 (e.g. metal trunking)
- straw, small screw and pin
- small pieces of paper of known mass, e.g. graph paper squares

Activity 3. Structures activity/circus
See Student Book page 120, Figure 4 for apparatus.
- 3 spring balances
- 3 clamp stands
- 3 G-clamps
- string
- beam
- weights

Activity 4. Stability of brick towers
- Lego® bricks
- board and supports

⚠ Safety

Care is needed when handling the structures in Activity 3 as they can become unstable. Students need to be careful of falling masses.

Unit 13 – Investigating scientific questions

The atomic world

pp 122–123

Curriculum link

NC PoS: Sc1:1a–c
Framework: SE1
QCA SoW: 9M Investigating Scientific Questions
Prior learning:

Most students will have done some investigation work at KS2, and at KS3 their skills are developed and extended.

Lesson guidance

Starter suggestions
- This lesson is on the development throughout history of the atom model used to describe matter. Studying the atom has led to tremendous benefits and great tragedies for humankind.
- Start by summarising the main ideas about atoms that students should already understand. Then get them to consider *evidence* for what they know about atoms. This is hard for students to recall, but evidence is the key idea to discuss in this lesson, and the key question 'What is scientific evidence?'

Development
- *Early ideas.* The Ancient Greeks, thinkers and not experimentalists, had the simple idea of an ultimate building block for matter.
- *Evidence of atoms.* Thinking about chemical compounds shows how useful the atomic building block idea is. Boyle's simple gas law can be very neatly explained using the idea of an atomic or molecular unit. Explain that the sign of a good scientific model is that it simplifies thinking, provides explanations for experimental data and can be used to suggest further experimental tests.
- *Activity 1.* Pursuing the gas theme, students experience the reduction of volume causing increasing pressure. Draw out, through discussion and aided by diagrams on board, how collisions between the walls of a container and gas particles may explain the observed pressure. This is quite an abstract notion for some, but other students will enjoy the exercise.
- *Brownian motion* can be demonstrated, and will help students to visualise tiny, randomly moving particles. Emphasise that it's large smoke particles that they see moving, not atoms or molecules.
- *Activity 2, Worksheet 52.* The overall idea is to show how physics models develop and change as experiments throw up new evidence that has to be explained. Nothing is set in tablets of stone. Answers: Q2 Height calculated from volume of oil drop and area of layer on water. Q3 Throwing tennis balls into the pile and observing angles at which those that hit the weight ricochet will indicate the iron weight's size and shape.

- *Demonstrate the electrolysis of water* to exemplify the atomic/molecular particle idea. Many students will have heard of H_2O, and the evidence for this can be seen in this experiment.
- *The oil drop experiment* can be demonstrated if possible. It shows how ingenious experiments give a good idea about details of a model.
- *Probing with projectiles.* Development of the atomic model speeded up in modern times – from 1905 onwards. To begin a discussion on scattering experiments, get the students to imagine a haystack covering a pile of cannonballs. Bullets are then used to 'probe' the haystack for its internal features. Analysing how the bullets scatter (they could be detected in sand traps), gives information about structures that cannot be seen. Then explain that scientists 'fired' subatomic particles at samples of matter. The scientists observed the way that these particles scattered from the samples and created models about the internal structure of matter.

Plenary and homework suggestions
- A good plenary exercise is for students to make a *PowerPoint* or a poster presentation on Rutherford. If students use *PowerPoint* and research on the web, you will be able to address the issue of quoting reference material, rather than students just cutting and pasting from the work of others.

Differentiation/extension
- Faster students might like to make a chart of scale, from the size of a human, through cells, molecules, atoms, the nucleus. The *Scientific American*-derived 'Powers of 10' video is excellent for this.

Technician notes
Activity 1. Compressing a gas
- plastic syringe, 10 cm³ or 20 cm³, outlet blocked

Demonstrating Brownian motion
- microscope (low power), smoke cell
- strong light source and lens to focus

Demonstrations to support particle model
Electrolysis of water:
- standard electrolysis equipment, power source
Rayleigh's oil drop experiment:
- oil drop on wire
- lycopodium powder to scatter on water

Unit 13 – Investigating scientific questions

Revising fair testing

pp 124–125

Curriculum link

NC PoS: Sc1:2a–p
Framework: SE2–SE7
QCA SoW: 9M Investigating Scientific Questions
Prior learning: See Teaching Resource 1, Investigation planning sheets, pp. xvi–xvii, and Teaching Resource 2, Investigation support sheets, pages xii–xiii.

Lesson guidance

Starter suggestions

- Most of the work in Sc1 physics will involve fair test investigations. There are other sorts of investigation, but these may be more easily tackled at this stage in Sc2 and Sc3 contexts. Using the board, collect together class ideas about what making a fair test involves.
- The pendulum experiment is a simple enough idea for this discussion. Get small groups to spend no longer than 10 minutes to plan this investigation, then ask groups to present their plans.

Development

- *Planning*. This section summarises the main ideas involved for many types of investigation. Using Q and A, develop the idea of independent and dependent variables, with examples.
- 🖩 Look at curved and straight-line graphs and show how the shape gives information on the relationship between the variables. You could project several graphs on the OHP for this purpose. The AKSIS material from ASE is particularly good in helping to teach graph interpretation.
- *Observing* and *Analysing*. Using the pendulum context, get groups to record data. Groups can measure the oscillation time for different lengths of pendulum. Here is an opportunity to discuss repeat measurements, minimising error, and 'range of data' issues. A lesson could be spent on these aspects alone.
- 🖱 After graphs are drawn using spreadsheets, shapes can be analysed. The curves obtained will be full of interesting discussion points. The idea of an inverse relation will be too difficult for most students at KS3, so the discussion should focus on how the slope of the graph changes for the range of data collected.
- 🖱 *Activity 1*. Supply the students with a spreadsheet file of straight-line data with artificial errors added. They plot the data but don't use any

line fits. Then they should draw in by hand several fits to the data. If the errors you have introduced are large, you may see students drawing curves. This is not a bad thing. Take the opportunity to point out that part of the analysing skill is to use physics ideas to anticipate the shapes of graphs. The lines can then be compared with the data, and the outcomes of this comparison discussed further.

- *Evaluating*. Investigation is not a linear process as presented here. Each stage is influenced by all the others. The fair testing process is a closed feedback loop and, as the students get better at investigating, this will become apparent to them. Draw their attention to the Investigation Support sheets on pages xv and xvi of Teacher Resources Books 1, 2 and 3.
- Students need to realise that their data will contain errors, and that this is natural. Perfect experiments are impossible! What is required is to report all data, discuss how their experiment is limited and how it could be improved; also to take sensible amounts of repeat measurements. In the evaluation stage they can show why they took the number of repeats they did. Knowing the limitations on accuracy of measurement is difficult at this stage. But simple rules about limitations on measuring length, time and temperature can be discussed. The three 'questions to keep in mind' are useful to start with.

Plenary and homework suggestions

- If students write up an aspect of the pendulum experiment, you will be able to give personal feedback to the class.

Technician notes
Pendulum oscillation times
- pendulums (different lengths)
- clamp stand
- stopwatch

Activity 1. Drawing a graph from data
- spreadsheet file of data with artificial errors

Unit 13 – Investigating scientific questions

Power for satellites

pp 126–127

Curriculum link

NC PoS: Sc4:1a-c; Sc1:2a–p
Framework: SE2–SE7
QCA SoW: 9M Investigating Scientific Questions
Prior learning: The students will need to be familiar with KS3 circuit models.

Lesson guidance

Starter suggestions

- You will need to revise basic circuit ideas, with the class using voltmeters and ammeters and drawing circuit diagrams. The ideas of voltage and current will be needed during the analysis stage.
- 🖱 Web research will allow students to understand the usefulness of solar cells.
- Playing with the cell to get ideas is important as a start, and will enable you to find out which groups will need a lot of help.

Development

- *Planning* and *Observing*. Most students will have lots of ideas and you will need to narrow things down, maybe by providing the question to be investigated and identifying key variables.
- *Activity 1* will get things moving the right way. After students have finished, summarise findings and make sure every group has a clear circuit diagram.
- Discuss what brightness may mean. (Lux or lumens may have been encountered before.) The key point is that in this investigation we want a simple measure of brightness only. Controlling bulb power or changing the bulb-to-panel distance are ways to control energy per second per unit area on to the solar cell.
- *Activity 2*. Students need to gather good data and, in that connection, now is the time to talk about range of variable values and repeat measurements. The idea of error needs careful discussion. Counter the notion that their imperfection has ruined the experiment. This will be important at evaluation stage.
- *Evaluating*. This stage needs careful orchestration if the students are inexperienced investigators.
- Some of the questions posed in the Student Book can be discussed.

Plenary and homework suggestions

- Just writing up is probably too difficult. Instead, small exercises are more useful, such as asking students to sketch and discuss a light intensity versus voltage output graph. Producing a data table and graphs with curves sketched carefully is also important.

Technician notes
Starter. Revising basic current ideas

- voltmeter
- ammeter
- power supply
- connecting wires
- solar cell

See Figures 1 and 2 on pages 126 and 127 for experimental set-up.

- variable power supply connected to bulb
- voltmeter
- solar cell connected to second voltmeter

Unit 13 – Investigating scientific questions

Squash balls pp 128–129

Curriculum link

NC PoS: Sc4:5d–g; Sc1:2a–p
Framework: SE2–SE7
QCA SoW: 9M Investigating Scientific Questions

Students will need to consolidate the idea of energy conservation. The fact that energy becomes dissipated as thermal energy should be discussed thoroughly before they begin work.

Lesson guidance

Starter suggestions

■ Try bouncing a cold squash ball and one heated in a water bath. Draw out energy ideas that will be useful for analysis in this investigation. Bounce height error can be discussed, without giving away too much about variables that students might consider.

Development

■ The investigation is quite focused for students who are inexperienced investigators or who might need careful guidance.

■ 🖩 🖱 Students should use spreadsheets to tabulate and process data. Graph drawing by hand and on computer should be encouraged.

■ *Planning and observing*. After groups have framed their question, ask them to discuss the ideas suggested in the planning and observing section of the text. They need to choose variables for investigation. Alternatively, they can be given a free choice of variables to investigate with no guidance. This is exciting, but needs planning so that no one is left floundering.

■ *Activity 1*. The bounce height error is a good opportunity to get the students used to dealing with simple length measurement error. Students are not likely to notice that the balls warm up during the course of their experiments. Squashing them violently and repeatedly with their hands will get the balls warm, however!

■ *Analysing*. This will allow you to discuss energy conservation with thermal dissipation. This is best done as a class discussion, gathering information from all groups and assembling the story on the board for all students to comment on.

■ *Evaluating*. The class needs to discuss the usual issues of variable range and number of repeat measurements. Some students will not have taken a large range of drop heights, and repeat measurements will be inadequate in number for such an error-prone data set. Using video cameras is useful for this investigation.

■ 📖 *Activity 2*. This is an important activity and you should look carefully at each group's attempt. Individual feedback is required.

Plenary and homework suggestions

■ How could the temperature of the squash ball be changed and its effect on bounce height determined? This is a good question for planning homework, and by now the students will have plenty of ideas to help them tackle this work.

Differentiation/extension

■ Faster students can be given this investigation to tackle on their own over a couple of double periods. The response can be very exciting. Others will need step-by-step guidance.

Technician notes
Starter demonstration and investigation of squash ball behaviour
Be on hand for special requests during the investigation.

■ selection of squash balls
■ water bath
■ meter ruler
■ clamp stand
■ video camera if webcam is available

Unit 1 – Inheritance and selection

Here are their Mum and Dad

This is Danny with his sister Isabel

List the characteristics Danny and Isabel have each inherited from their Dad. Repeat for their Mum.

② New varieties

Q1 What advantage would there be in producing a new variety of wheat that has a shorter stem?

_____

_____

Q2 What advantage would there be in producing a new variety of wheat with a larger 'ear'?

_____

_____

Q3 A plant grower wants to breed a better rose bush from the two shown above. Draw a diagram to show what the new variety of plant could look like.

Q4 What did the plant breeder have to do to get the new variety?

_____

_____

Q5 What other features that you can't see in the picture might the plant breeder have wanted in the new variety?

_____

_____

Unit 1 – Inheritance and selection

There are lots of farms that rear cattle for their milk, for their meat or to produce leather. Not all of these farms will have a bull because sperm from one bull can be used to fertilise a large number of cows.

Which bull?

Sperm is taken from a prize bull and frozen.

Q1 Discuss how you think the judges decide which bull should be given the prize.

A vet injects the sperm into a large number of cows. This means the genes from one bull will be passed on to many offspring.

Each calf will have characteristics from the same bull but a different cow.

Q2 Which characteristics might the farmer want the calves to inherit from the bull?

Which cow?

The farmer can also choose which cows have the most desirable characteristics and use them for breeding.

* Some of the ova (eggs) from these cows can be removed from their ovaries and then mixed with sperm in a test tube.

* Any ova that are fertilised can be injected back into a cow.

* The cow does not have to be the one that donated the ova.

* When the cow gives birth, she will start to produce milk. This milk can be put into bottles for us to drink.

Q3 Which group of vertebrates does the cow belong to? Explain how you know this.

 # Investigating whether frozen peas weigh less than fresh peas

pp 26–27

Collecting data

1. Collect a sample of 10 fresh peas.

2. Use a very sensitive digital balance to measure the mass of each one accurately. Alternatively, if each pea is too light to register on the balance, measure all 10 peas at once and divide by 10 to calculate an average.

3. Record the results in the table.

4. Repeat with a sample of 10 frozen peas.

Peas in the sample	Mass (g) when fresh	Mass (g) when frozen
1		
2		
3		
4		
5		
6		
7		
8		
9		
10		

Interpreting your results

1. For more reliable data, collate all of the class results together.

2. Calculate the average mass for each type of pea.

3. Work out the range of masses for each type of pea – the lightest to the heaviest.

4. Plot a graph as shown below:

Q1 Are the average masses the same or different? If they are different, is it significant or are they quite close?

Q2 Do you think the sample size was large enough to give you reliable results? Explain your answer.

Q3 Is there any overlap in the ranges of masses between the two types of pea?

Q4 Do you have sufficient data to conclude that frozen peas weigh less than fresh peas?

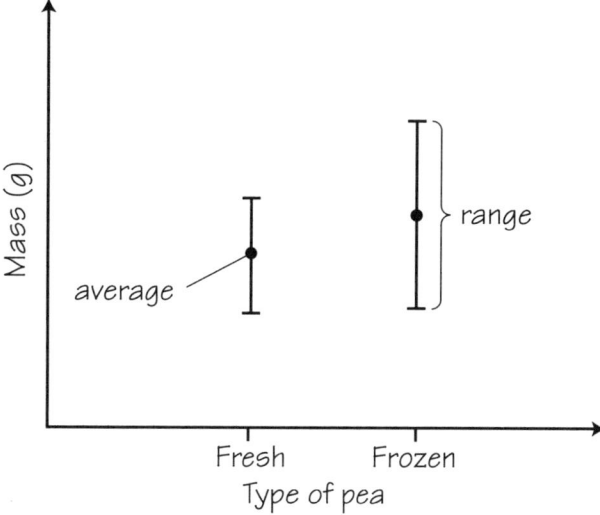

Unit 1 – Inheritance and selection

5 Growing cuttings

Unit 1 – Inheritance and selection

Follow the instructions below to grow a new plant from a cutting.

1. Choose a healthy plant that has lots of branching side shoots.
   A geranium, begonia or tomato shoot usually works well.

2. Cut a side shoot from the parent plant, cutting as close to the main stem as you can.

3. Place the cutting in a conical flask with the cut end of the stem in water.

4. If necessary, plug the top of the flask gently with cotton wool to support the cutting so that it does not slide inside.

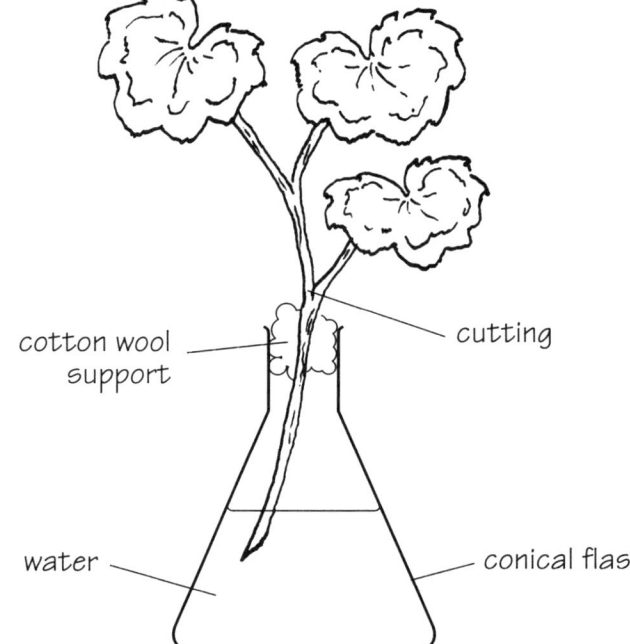

cotton wool support

cutting

water

conical flask

5. Give the cutting time to grow new roots.

6. Replant the cutting in a mixture of soil and compost.

7. Water it regularly.

8. Hopefully, the roots will develop further and your cutting will grow into a new plant.

> **Remember**
>
> The cutting has grown from the cells of the parent plant, which means it is **cloned**.

6 Measure your fitness

pp 30–31

1. How many days have you had off school due to illness in the last month?

   _____

2. Work in pairs. One of you times a minute on the stopwatch, while the other counts how many times they breathe out. This is your breathing rate at rest. Write it down.

   _____

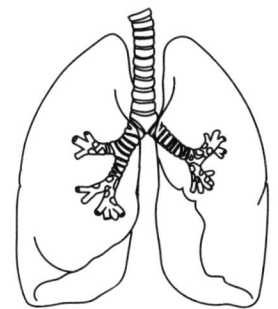

3. Do squat jumps for 1 minute – squat down so that your bottom touches your heels and then jump into the air. Measure your breathing rate after exercise.

   _____

4. Measure your resting heart rate by taking your pulse. Find your pulse in your wrist or neck and count the number of beats in one minute.

   _____

5. Start the stopwatch and begin running on the spot. Keep going for as long as you can and then write down the time.

   _____

6. Measure your heart rate again after exercising in step 5.

   _____

7. Hold a 1 kg mass at full arm's length. Time how long you can hold it in this position before your muscles tire and you have to put the weight down.

   _____

8. Work in pairs. Bend forward from the hips but keep the legs straight. Try to touch your toes if possible. Your partner will measure the distance between your fingertips and your toes.

   _____

9. Describe what you see in the picture. ⟶

   _____

* Display your results to these activities – decide the best way to do this to show them clearly.

* Interpret the results. What do they tell you about your fitness levels?

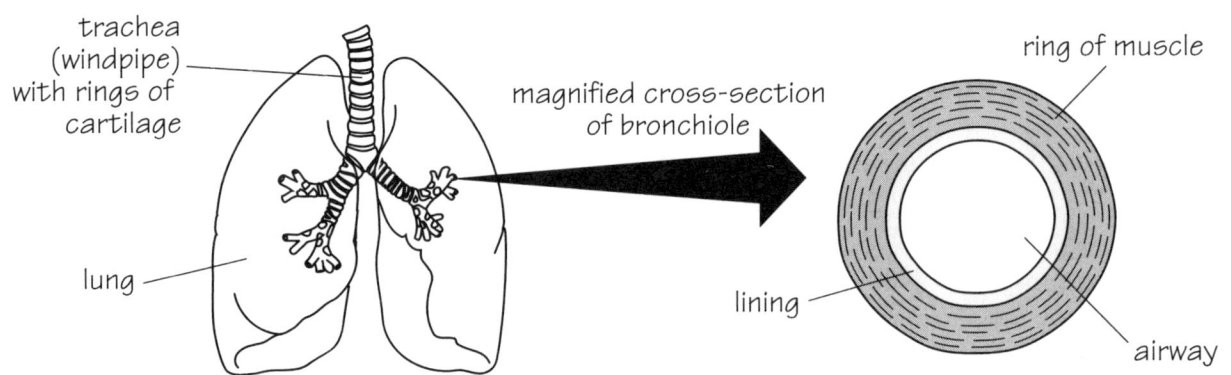

trachea (windpipe) with rings of cartilage

magnified cross-section of bronchiole

ring of muscle

lung

lining

airway

Nowadays, about 1 in 10 children suffer from asthma. It is the biggest cause of absence from school.

The number of cases of asthma has increased dramatically over the last 20 years. Scientists are unsure of the reason for this, but these are a couple of theories:

✱ **Dust mites**. They live in carpets, curtains and mattresses feeding off our dead skin. When houses have central heating, the mites can survive all year round. Their droppings may trigger an asthma attack.

✱ **Traffic pollution**. The increase in the number of cars on our roads may be the cause of asthma.

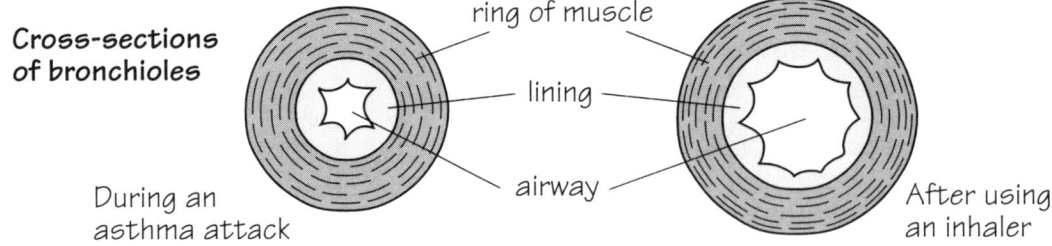

Cross-sections of bronchioles

ring of muscle

lining

airway

During an asthma attack

After using an inhaler

Use the pictures and the words below to help you complete the sentences.

During an asthma attack, the muscles 1_____ and the lining becomes 2_____. This 3_____ the airways causing you to breathe 4_____.

The chemical in the inhaler 5_____ the muscles so the airways are opened up. This allows more 6_____ to enter and leave the lungs. The breathing 7_____ returns to normal.

air   faster   rate   swollen
contract   narrows   relaxes

Match the drugs on the left to their effects on the body by drawing a straight line between the boxes.

Caffeine

Nicotine

Amphetamine

Alcohol

Cocaine

LSD

Cannabis

Heroin

A. Makes you more alert and gives a feeling of being 'high'. You may become confused and find it very difficult to breathe.

B. Person becomes more relaxed even though the heart rate is increased slightly.

C. Increases the heart rate and the blood pressure.

D. Wakes you up, stimulates the heart and increases the ability to think clearly.

E. The senses are distorted so that sight/sound/smell/taste/ hearing can be confused. It may cause vomiting or shivering. Makes the eyes red and dries out the mouth.

F. Gives a feeling of intense pleasure. Addiction develops very rapidly.

G. Makes you very active and 'speeds' you up. You may become very anxious or have hallucinations.

H. Makes you happy, then you lose your inhibitions and have increased reaction times. Speech and walking become difficult.

Unit 2 – Fit and healthy

9 Planning an investigation – Does alcohol affect reaction time?

pp 36–37

Framing a question

Q1 What is the independent variable?

Q2 What is the dependent variable?

Q3 What is the relationship you are investigating?

Preliminary work

You can use a ruler to measure reaction times.

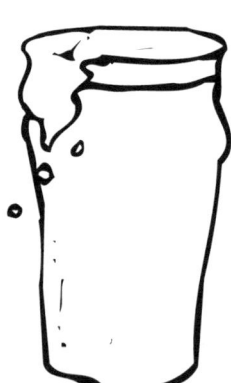

1. A partner holds a 1 m ruler at the top and you position your thumb and forefinger at the zero mark without actually touching the ruler. When your partner shouts 'Now', they will drop the ruler and you must catch it as soon as possible. Measure where your finger and thumb touch the ruler – the higher up the ruler you have caught it, the slower your reaction time.

Q4 Does it matter which hand you use, or if your eyes are open or closed, or what time of day it is?

Explain the plan

Q5 Describe, step by step, how you would use the ruler technique to find out whether alcohol affects reaction times.

Q6 What safety precautions do you need to take?

Data collection

Q7 How will you make sure you measure accurately with the ruler?

Q8 How many times will you change the independent variable and how will you do this?

Q9 How many people should you test? What would be the size of your sample?

Fair test

Q10 Describe what you would need to keep the same throughout the experiment and how you would do this.

Prediction

Q11 What do you think will happen to people's reaction times in this investigation?

Q12 Explain the relationship you have predicted between alcohol and reaction times.

Improving the plan

Q13 Can you think of a different technique that measures your reaction time much more accurately?

Success for Schools: Science Book 3 – © Letts Educational 2004

10 Plants as producers

pp 38–39

Cut out the boxes below to position in the correct place on the diagram.

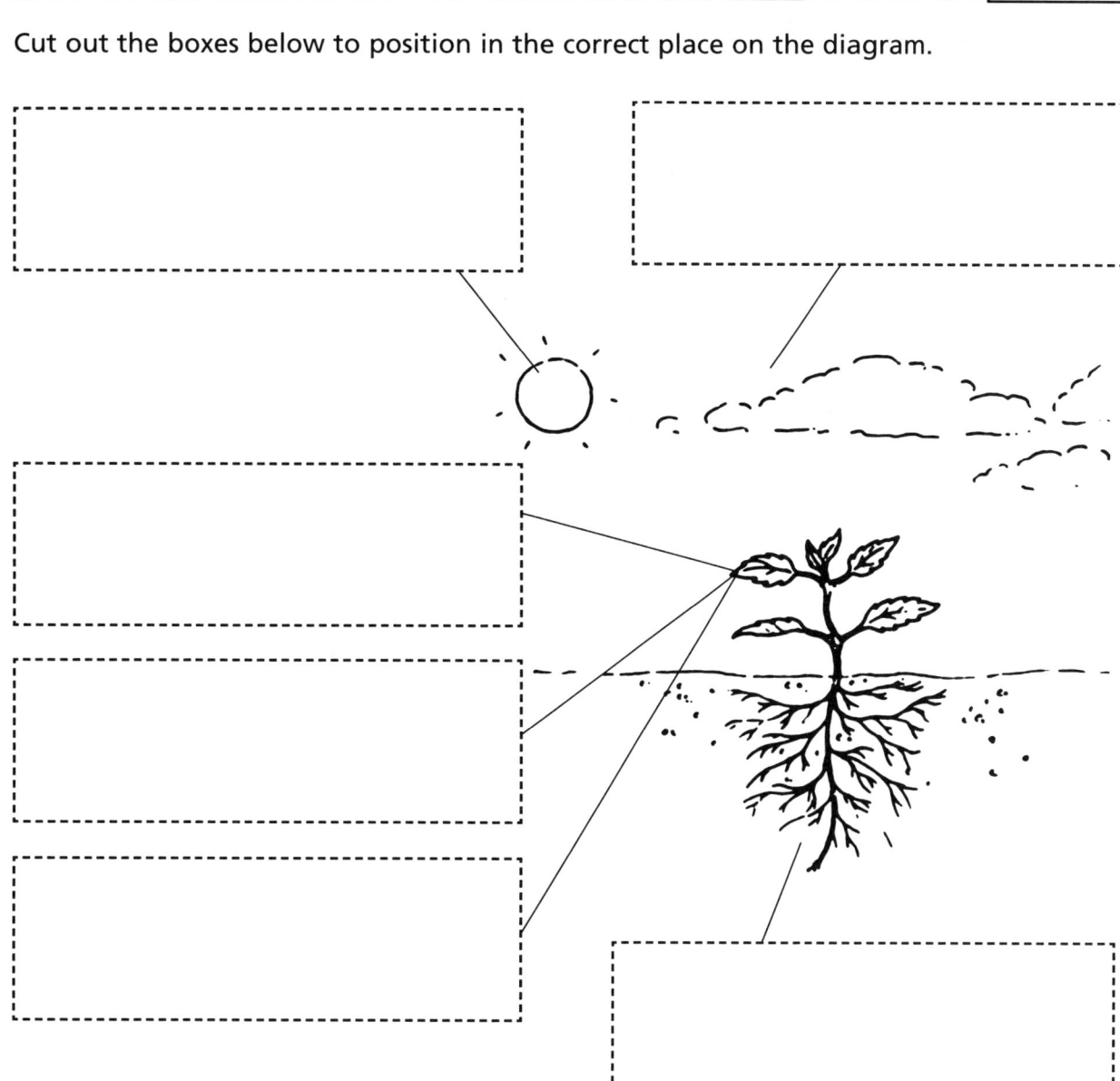

Organ where photosynthesis takes place	Absorb water – a raw material for photosynthesis
Where glucose is made	Provides the light energy for the chemical reaction
Absorb carbon dioxide – a raw material for photosynthesis	Where the oxygen goes that is made during photosynthesis

⑪ Experiment to test a leaf for starch

Follow the instructions carefully to find out whether your leaf has made glucose by photosynthesis and then changed it to starch for storage.

1. Set up a water bath over a Bunsen burner as shown in the diagram.

2. Add a fresh leaf to the water and let it boil for 1 minute. This softens the leaf and breaks open the cells.

3. Switch off the Bunsen burner and put it away.

4. Use forceps to take the leaf out of the water and put it into a boiling tube.

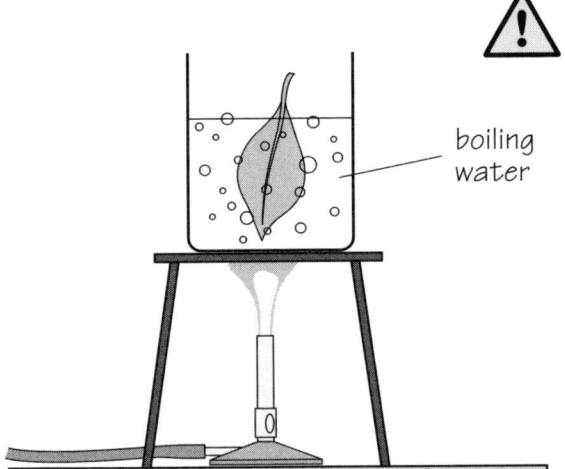

boiling water

5. Take the boiling tube to your teacher who will pour ethanol over the leaf.

6. Put the boiling tube into the water bath.

7. The ethanol removes the chlorophyll from the leaf, so you need to wait until the ethanol turns green and the leaf turns white.

8. Remove the leaf with the forceps and rinse it in the water bath to wash off the ethanol.

9. Gently lay the leaf out flat on a white tile and drip iodine solution onto the whole surface.

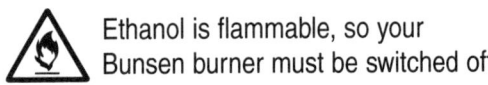
Ethanol is flammable, so your Bunsen burner must be switched off.

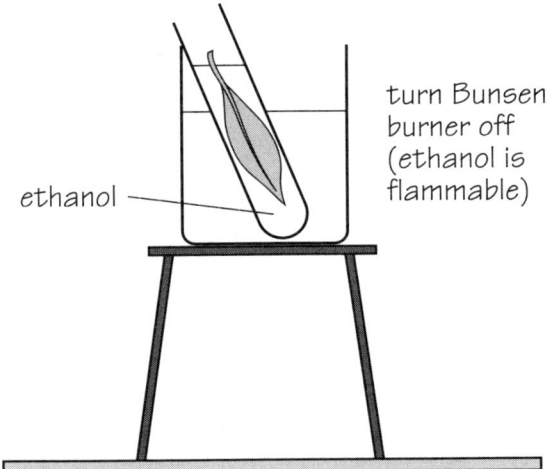

ethanol

turn Bunsen burner off (ethanol is flammable)

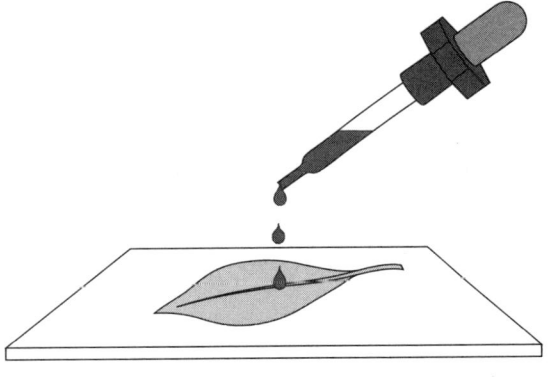

IODINE SOLUTION

10. Observe the areas that contain starch turning blue-black.

Success for Schools: Science Book 3 – © Letts Educational 2004

Unit 3 – Plants and photosynthesis

12 The effect of light intensity on the rate of photosynthesis

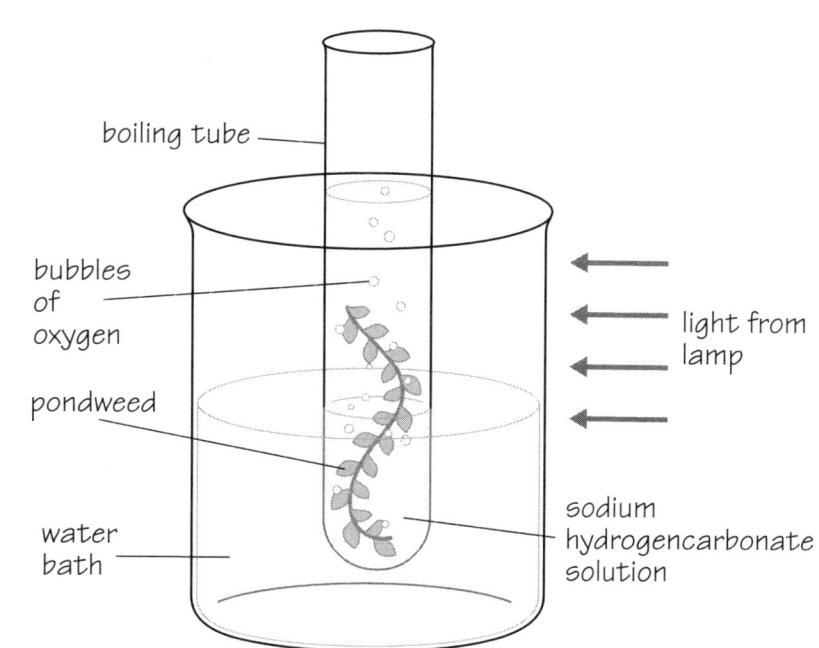

pp 42–43

In the experiment shown in the diagram:

* The **independent variable** is the intensity of light – positioning the lamp at different distances from the water bath changes this.

* The **dependent variable** is the rate of photosynthesis – this is measured by counting the number of oxygen bubbles for two minutes each time.

boiling tube

bubbles of oxygen

pondweed

water bath

light from lamp

sodium hydrogencarbonate solution

This table shows the results.

Distance of lamp from the water bath (cm)	Number of oxygen bubbles in two minutes
5	126
10	124
15	111
20	86
25	52

Q1 Draw a line graph of these results – remember that the independent variable goes along the horizontal axis and the dependent variable goes on the vertical axis.

Q2 What happens to the number of oxygen bubbles as the lamp is moved further away?

Q3 Use these results to write a sentence describing the relationship between light intensity and the rate of photosynthesis – this is your **conclusion**.

Q4 Look at the results for 5 cm and 10 cm. What do you think would happen if the lamp were moved even closer?

Q5 List any variables that would need to have been kept constant in this experiment for a fair test.

Unit 3 – Plants and photosynthesis

Crops of potatoes were grown in three different plots of land. Each plot was treated differently to investigate the effect of adding fertiliser. The fertiliser contained nitrates, phosphates and potassium, and this mixture of minerals is called NPK after the symbols of the important elements in them.

Interpret the results from the investigation and answer the questions below.

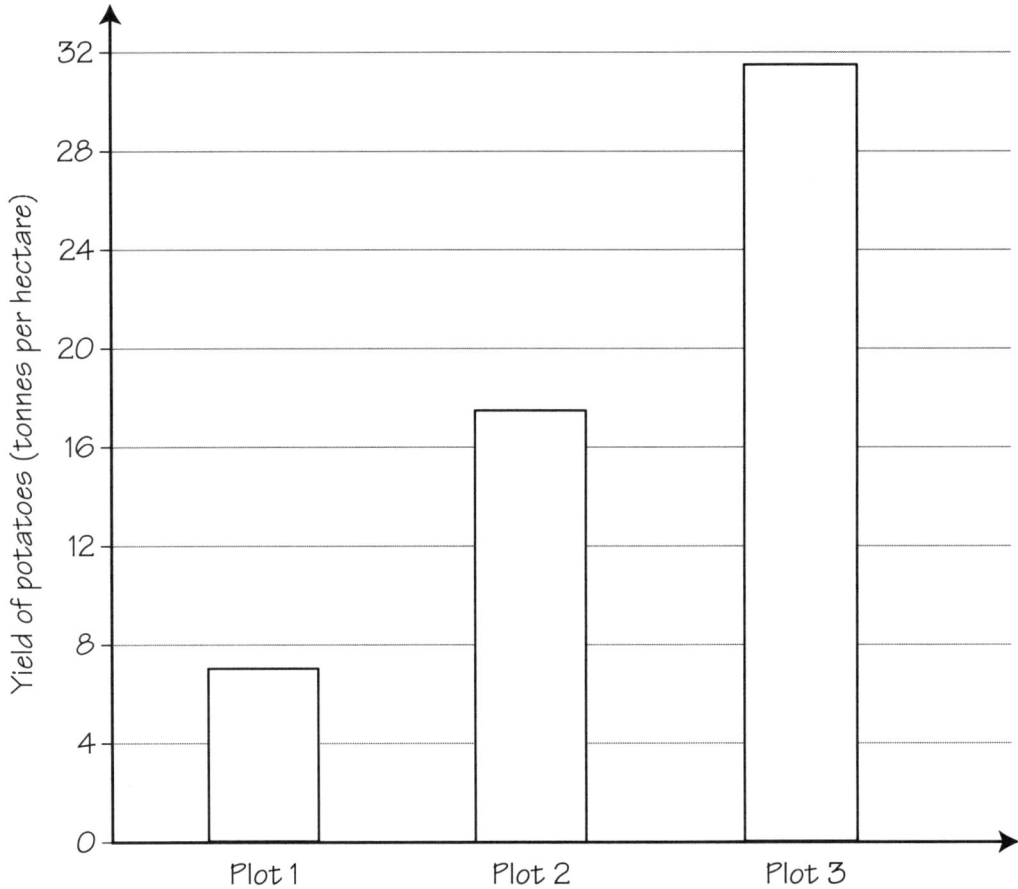

Q1 Match each plot to the treatment it received:

(a) Fertiliser added – N, P and K in equal amounts.

(b) Fertiliser added – 4 times more N than P and K.

(c) No fertiliser added.

Q2 Explain your decisions for question 1.

Q3 What was the reason for using a plot with no fertiliser added?

Q4 What difference was there in the yield of potatoes from Plot 1 compared to Plot 2?

Q5 Why is it necessary to add fertiliser to the soil when growing crops?

Q6 Extension: Find out why growing peas and beans every couple of years instead of potatoes every year can actually increase the potato yield.

Unit 3 – Plants and photosynthesis

14 The balance between photosynthesis and respiration

pp 46–47

Use the words below to fill in the gaps.
Each word can be used more than once.

During photosynthesis, plants take in _____ _____ gas

through pores in the leaf called _____. The _____ absorb

water, which is transported to the leaves through the _____ vessels.

Chlorophyll is the green colour in the leaf that absorbs _____ energy

that brings about the chemical reaction.

The word equation for photosynthesis is:

$$\underline{\hspace{2cm}} \; \underline{\hspace{2cm}} + \underline{\hspace{2cm}} \xrightarrow[\text{chlorophyll}]{\text{sunlight}} \underline{\hspace{2cm}} + \text{oxygen}$$

The _____ is released into the air.

Chlorophyll is contained in the _____, which are concentrated in the

_____ cells.

All other organisms depend on photosynthesis because they need oxygen for

_____. The plants, which release oxygen and use up carbon dioxide, are

the _____ at the start of the food chain.

The word equation for respiration is:

Glucose + _____ → carbon dioxide + _____

carbon dioxide	**glucose**	**respiration**	**xylem**
chloroplasts	**producers**	**oxygen**	**stomata**
	roots	**palisade** **water**	**sunlight**

Cut out the boxes below and stick in the correct place on the diagram. Box 3 has been done for you.

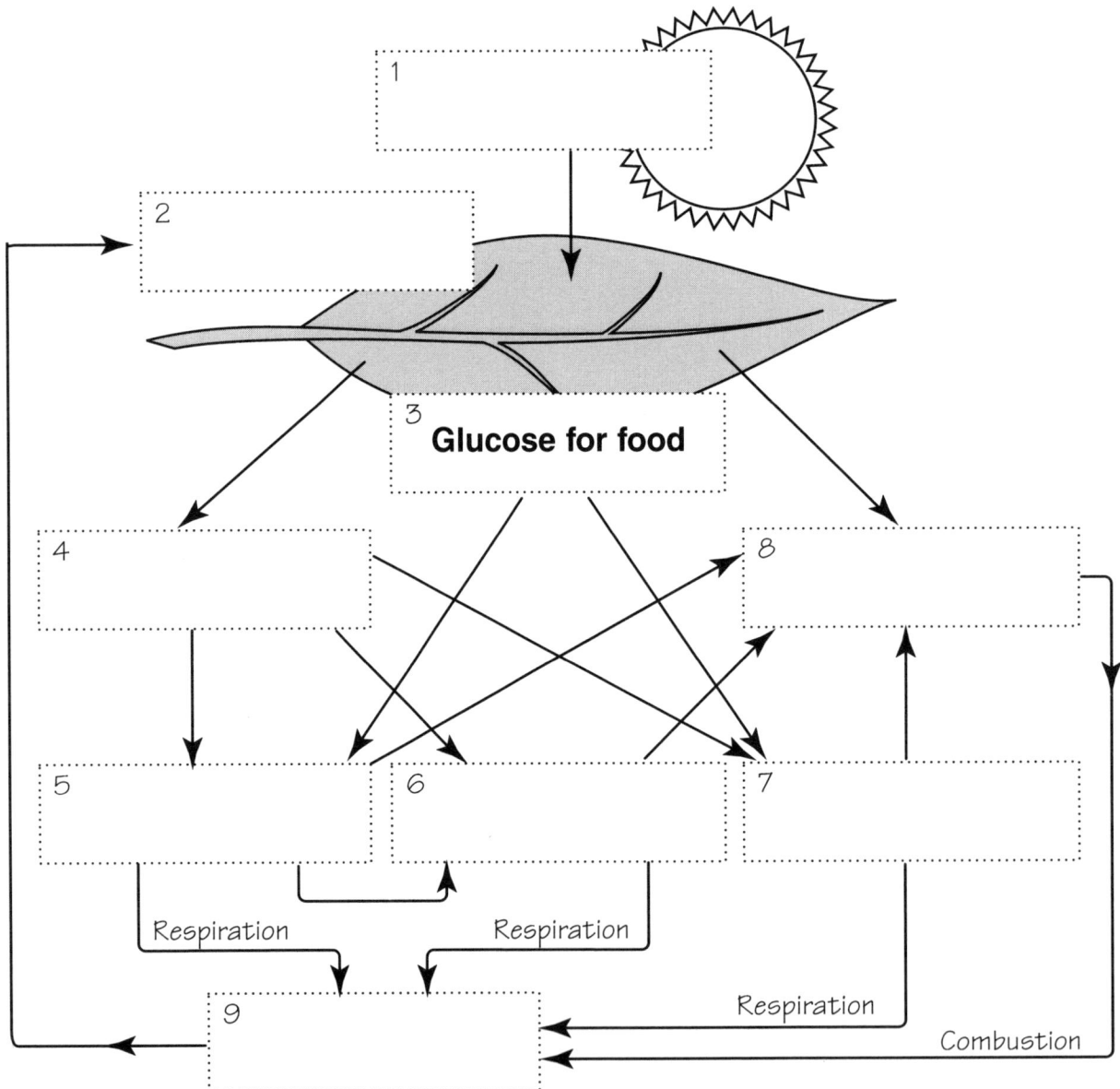

3 **Glucose for food**

Respiration

Respiration

Respiration

Combustion

Carbon dioxide for photosynthesis	Eaten by herbivores	Eaten by carnivores
Eaten by omnivores	Oxygen for respiration	Glucose for food
Light energy	May form fossil fuels	PHOTOSYNTHESIS

A food chain shows the transfer of energy from one organism to another. Energy is lost at each stage of the food chain.

Use the diagram to help you answer the questions below.

Q1 What percentage of light energy is lost before reaching the first organism?

Q2 What percentage of the energy absorbed by plants do they use to stay alive?

Q3 If the cow obtains 10% of the energy from the grain, how many kilograms does it eat?

Q4 In what ways does the cow use 90% of the energy it has eaten?

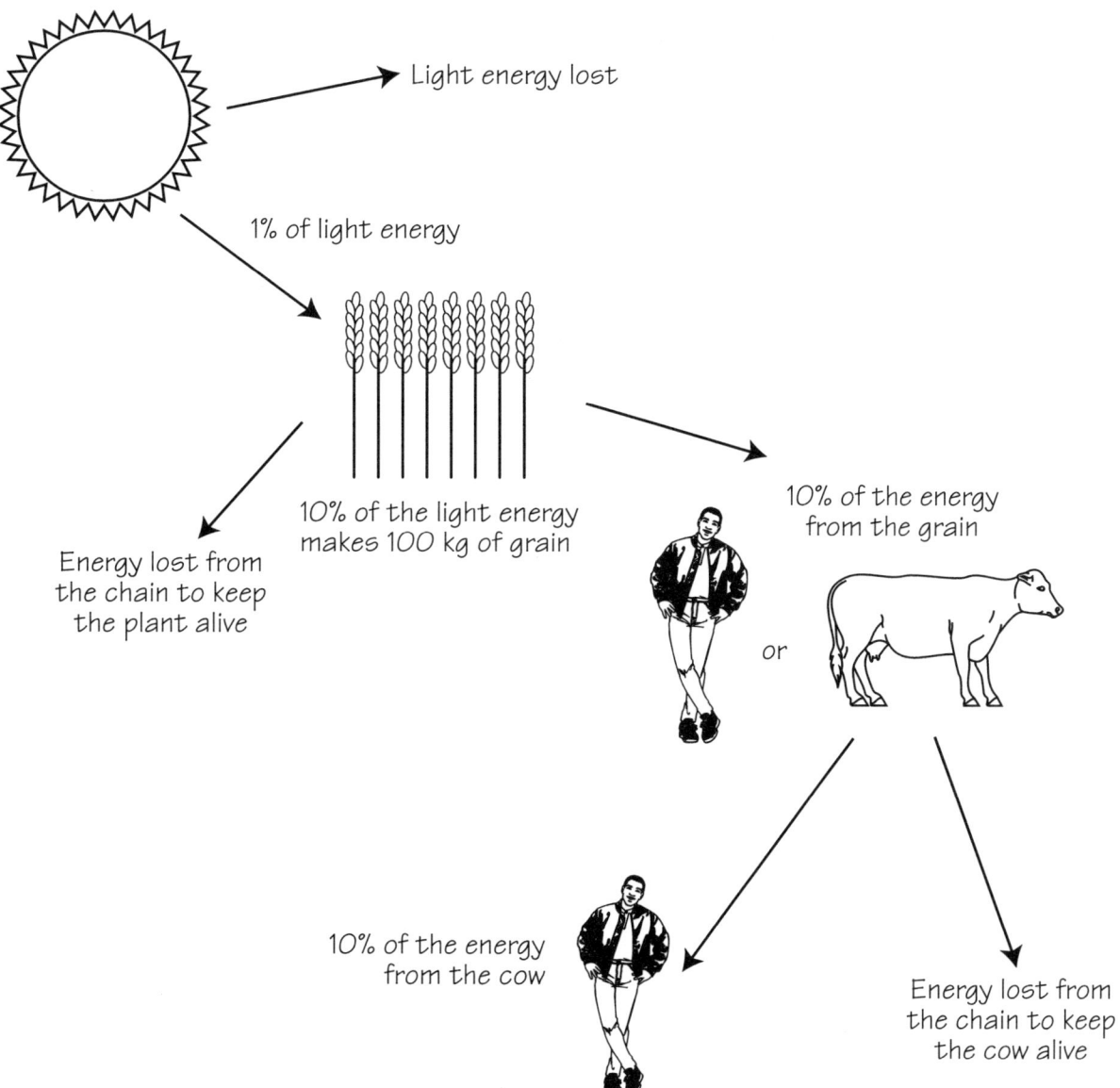

Light energy lost

1% of light energy

Energy lost from the chain to keep the plant alive

10% of the light energy makes 100 kg of grain

10% of the energy from the grain

or

10% of the energy from the cow

Energy lost from the chain to keep the cow alive

Q5 If the human obtains 10% of the energy from the cow, how many kilograms of meat does he eat?

Q6 Use the answers to questions 3, 4 and 5 to explain why vegetarians are obtaining a greater percentage of the light energy than meat-eaters.

Q7 Use your knowledge about balanced diets to explain the disadvantages of being vegetarian.

Success for Schools: Science Book 3 – © Letts Educational 2004

Unit 4 – Plants for food

71

17 Investigating the effect of nitrate on plant growth

pp 52–53

The **independent variable** is the concentration of nitrate.

The **dependent variable** is the size of the plant population.

Q1 Describe the relationship being investigated.

> Dissolving different quantities in water alters the nitrate concentration.

> Duckweed can be used as the plant to measure the effects the nitrate has on the size of its population. Each plant has just one leaf – so counting the number of leaves gives you the size of the population.

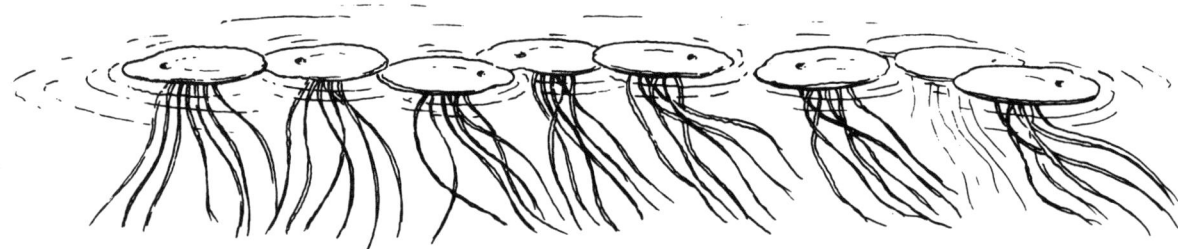

Q2 What apparatus would you need to carry out this investigation?

Q3 Describe, step by step, the method you would use. Include:

(a) The number of different concentrations of nitrate to test.

(b) The control experiment and the reason you need it.

(c) The size of the sample you would use for reliable results.

(d) The variables to be kept constant for a fair test.

(e) Any hazards or risks and how to avoid them.

Q4 Draw the axes of a graph to show how you would display the data collected.

Q5 Make a prediction: What do you think the relationship will be between the independent and dependent variables?

Q6 Sketch a line on your graph to show what your predicted results would look like.

Q7 Explain your reasons for this prediction using your scientific knowledge about the effects of nitrate fertilisers.

Unit 4 – Plants for food

72

Q1 Draw a pyramid of numbers to represent this food chain.

grass ⟶ hens ⟶ foxes

Q2 Humans want the hens for themselves so they shoot a large number of the foxes. Draw the pyramid of numbers again to show the effects of this.

Q3 Draw a pyramid of numbers to represent this food chain.

cabbages ⟶ caterpillars ⟶ bluetits ⟶ hawks

Q4 Humans want the cabbages for themselves, so they use a chemical pesticide to kill some of the caterpillars. Draw the pyramid of numbers again to show the effects of this.

Q5 Draw two pyramids of numbers to represent both of the food chains in this web.

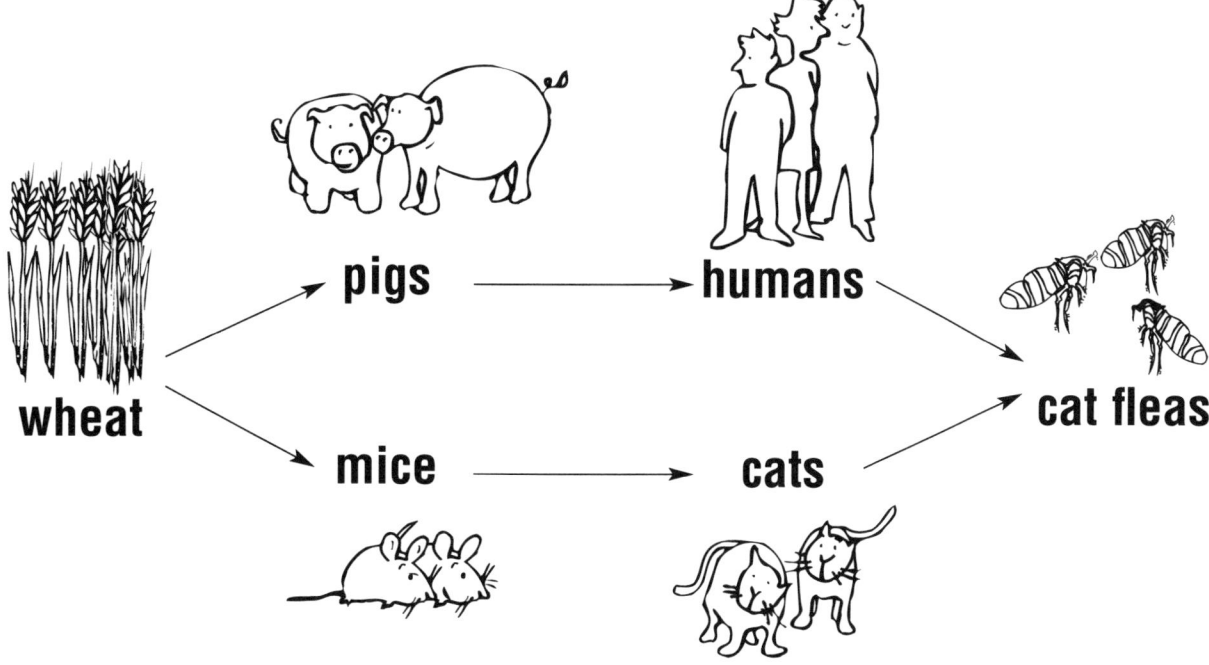

Q6 The humans trap and poison some of the mice. Draw the two pyramids again to show the effects of this.

Unit 4 – Plants for food

19 A deadly food chain

In the 1940s, an insecticide called DDT was made. Scientists believed it was the perfect way to kill insects such as crop pests and mosquitoes. Unfortunately, they did not know about **bioaccumulation**. DDT is persistent, so it builds up in the bodies of the insects and becomes more concentrated further up the food chain. For example:

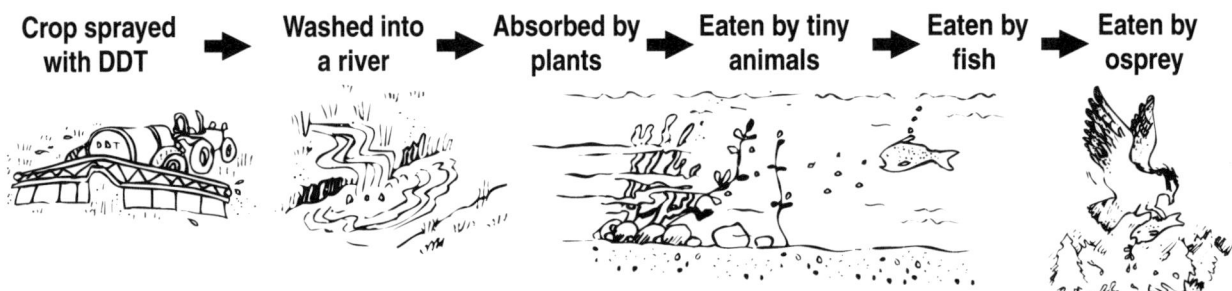

Crop sprayed with DDT → Washed into a river → Absorbed by plants → Eaten by tiny animals → Eaten by fish → Eaten by osprey

Q1 Which animal is the top predator in the food chain?

Q2 Draw a pyramid of numbers for this food chain.

Twenty years after the introduction of DDT, scientists noticed a drop in the numbers of birds of prey like the osprey. They began to gather evidence.

Q3 How much DDT was there in every million grams of grebe muscle?

Q4 Why is there more DDT in the grebes and herons, that feed on fish, than in the moorhens that feed on plants?

Q5 How much greater is the concentration of DDT in the sparrowhawks compared to the DDT concentration in the woodpigeons?

Q6 What does this tell you about their position in the food chain?

The scientists discovered that the DDT reduced the thickness of the eggshells.

Q7 What might happen to thin-shelled eggs in the nest?

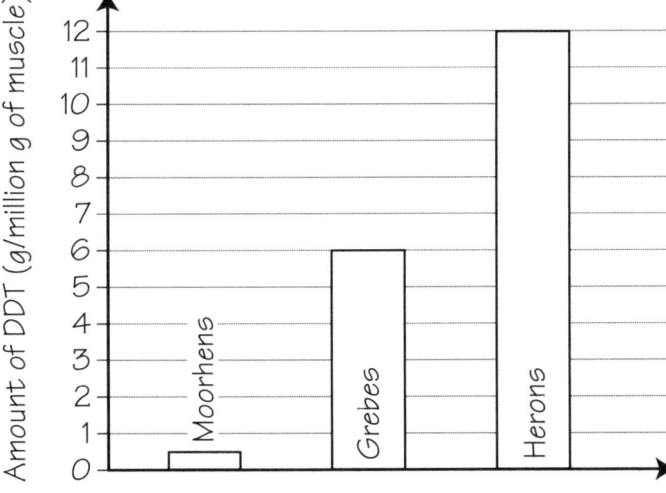

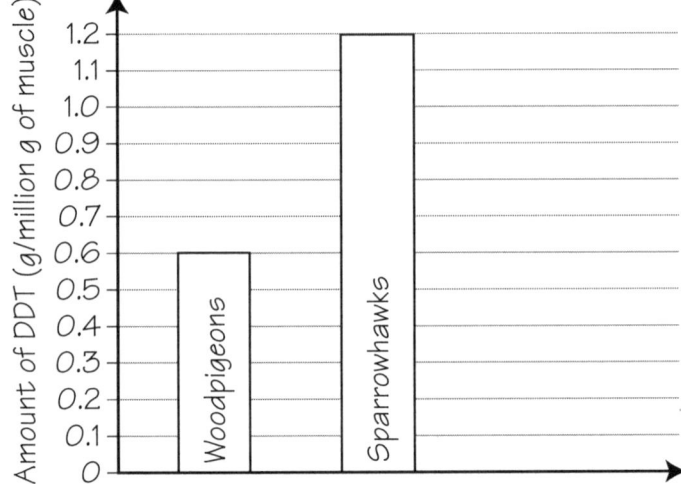

Metals and non-metals

You are going to compare the appearance and electrical conductivity of some metals and non-metals.

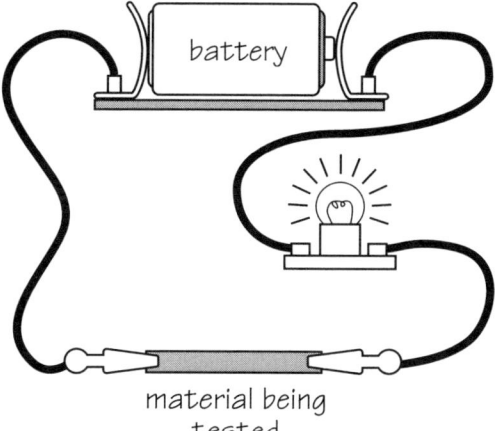

battery

material being tested

1. Use a battery, wires and a bulb to make a 'conductivity tester'.
2. Investigate the materials your teacher shows you. Make a table to record information about their appearance and whether or not they conduct electricity.

Q1 Why is graphite an unusual non-metal?

3. Find out whether **plastic coated** or **painted** metals conduct electricity.
4. Investigate different types of **packaging** by looking at the **appearance** and whether or not the materials **conduct electricity**. Which packaging contains metals? Find out what metals are used in packaging. What makes them good materials 'for the job'?

Looking closely at metals

Note: The higher the electrical conductivity value, the better the metal conducts. Density tells us how much a cubic centimetre of each metal weighs.

Metal	Melting point (°C)	Electrical conductivity (S)	Density (g/cm³)	Reactivity	Other
Aluminium	660	0.38	2.7	does not corrode	expensive, weak
Copper	1083	0.59	8.9	corrodes	expensive, weak
Iron	1535	0.10	7.9	corrodes	cheap, medium strength
Lithium	180	0.11	0.53	explosively reactive	expensive, very soft
Silver	961	0.62	10.5	corrodes slowly	very expensive, weak

Q2 Use data from the table to explain the following.

(a) Copper is used for underground electrical cables, but aluminium is used for overhead cables.

(b) Silver would be a good choice for electrical cables but in practice it is not used.

(c) Lithium has very few practical uses.

(d) Aluminium and copper are both used for making pans, but aluminium is used most.

(e) Iron is the most commonly used metal.

Unit 5 – Reactions of metals and metal compounds

Unit 5 – Reactions of metals and metal compounds

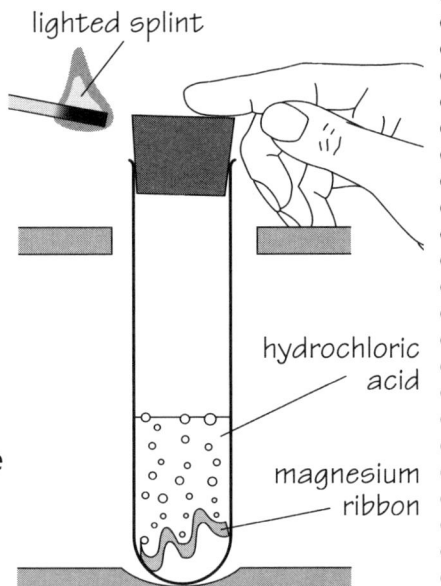

Reacting magnesium and hydrochloric acid

In this experiment you are going to find out what is made when magnesium reacts with hydrochloric acid.

1. Fill a test tube about half full of hydrochloric acid and stand it in a rack.
2. Add two small pieces of magnesium. Hold a bung *gently* in the top of the test tube until you can feel it pushing against your finger.
3. Remove the bung and quickly put a lighted splint into the test tube.

Q1 What happens? What does this tell you is being made?

4. Add more magnesium, one piece at a time, until the reaction stops. Keep the solution you have made.

Q2 How can you tell the reaction has stopped?

Q3 Why do you think the reaction stops?

lighted splint

hydrochloric acid

magnesium ribbon

What is left in the solution?

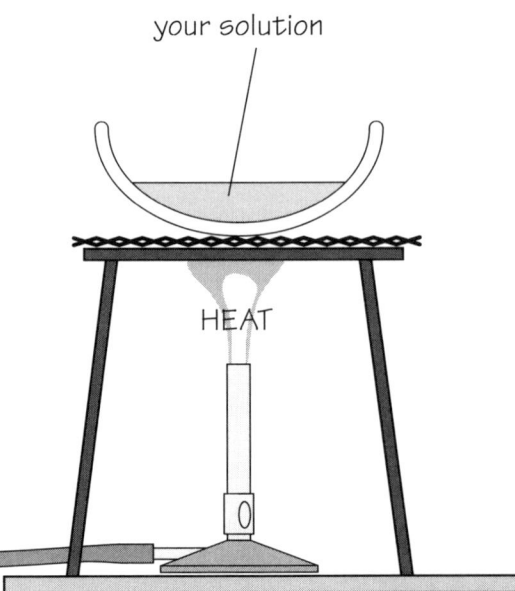

1. Pour your solution into an evaporating basin. Remove any left-over magnesium pieces using forceps.
2. Evaporate your solution. STOP HEATING when about two-thirds of the water has evaporated.

Q4 What do you see in the evaporating basin? What do you think this substance is?

Q5 Think about what you have seen happen.

   (a) What substances did you have at the start?

   (b) What substances were made in the reaction?

   (c) Write a word equation for the reaction.

   (d) If you had stopped adding magnesium in the middle of the experiment, what would have been left in the test tube?

your solution

HEAT

76

22 Making copper chloride

pp 62–63

The reaction for making copper chloride

You are going to make copper chloride by reacting different solids with hydrochloric acid. You will be using *either* **copper oxide** *or* **copper carbonate** *or* **malachite** (an ore of copper that contains copper carbonate).

1. During this experiment you need to make **observations** about what *changes you see* and what the *substances look like* as you see the changes happen. Decide how you will write these down clearly.
2. Use a measuring cylinder to measure 20 cm³ hydrochloric acid into a beaker.
3. Add your solid – your teacher will tell you which one to use – to the beaker, a little at a time.

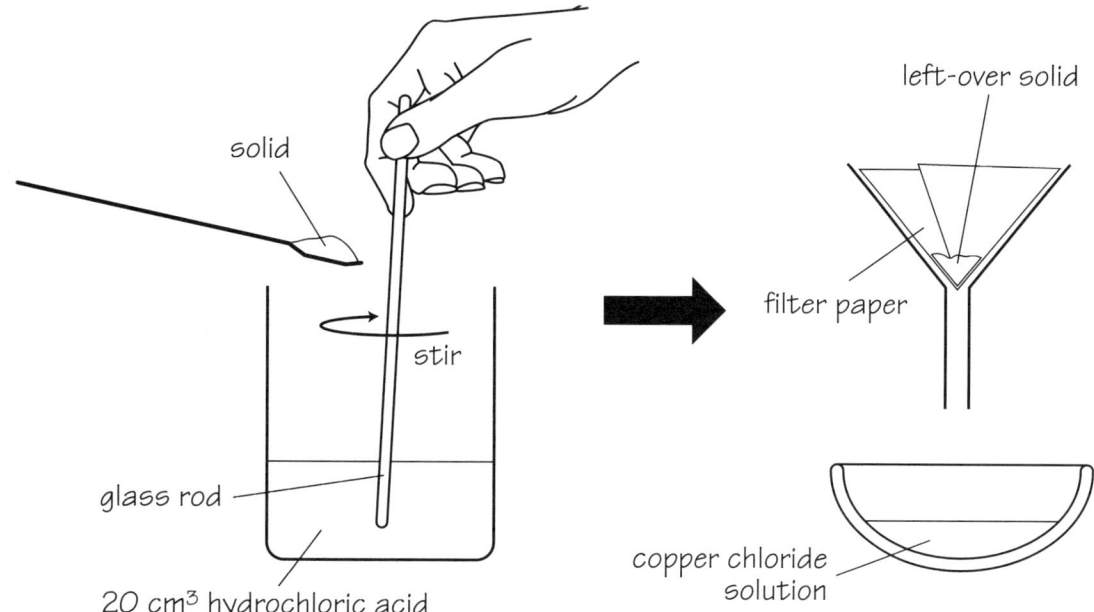

4. STOP adding the solid when you cannot see any more changes happening.
5. You will have added too much solid. Get this extra solid out by filtering it. You will be left with a solution of copper chloride.

Q1 What did you see that shows a chemical change has happened?

Q2 Apart from copper chloride, what else is made in the reaction? Try to write a word equation for the reaction.

Making copper chloride crystals

1. Evaporate your copper chloride solution in an evaporating basin. Remember to **stop heating** when you have about one-third of your solution left.
2. Compare your crystals with the ones that other groups have made.

Q3 Can you tell by looking at the crystals whether they were made using copper oxide, copper carbonate or malachite? Explain your answer.

Unit 5 – Reactions of metals and metal compounds

pp 64–65

How much sodium hydroxide do you need to add?

You are going to make sodium chloride by adding sodium hydroxide to hydrochloric acid.

1. Use a measuring cylinder to add 20 cm³ hydrochloric acid to a beaker standing on a white tile.
2. Add a few drops of Universal Indicator solution.
3. Rinse out the measuring cylinder, and fill it with 40 cm³ sodium hydroxide. (This will be more than you need.)

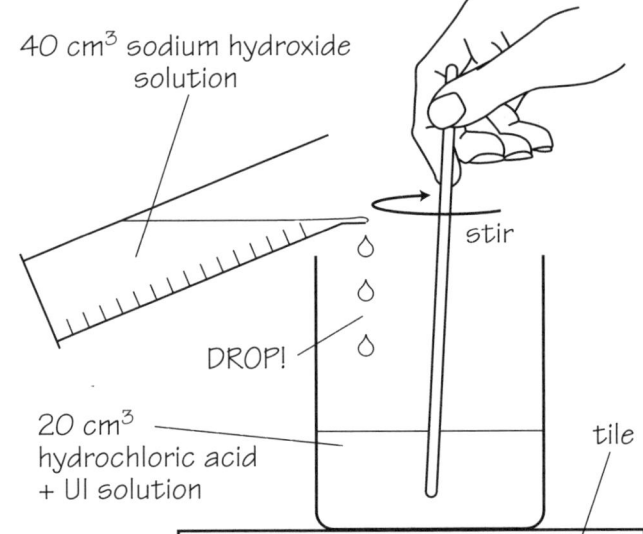

40 cm³ sodium hydroxide solution

stir

DROP!

20 cm³ hydrochloric acid + UI solution

tile

4. Add the sodium hydroxide, a very little at a time, to the beaker of acid. Keep stirring the acid.
5. **Stop** adding the sodium hydroxide when the mixture in the beaker turns purple.

Q1 How much sodium hydroxide is left in your measuring cylinder? How much have you added to the acid?

Making sodium chloride

When you make a **pure sample** of sodium chloride, you do not want any UI solution in your beaker – this is an 'impurity'. You have worked out how much sodium hydroxide will exactly neutralise 20 cm³ hydrochloric acid.

1. Repeat the experiment. This time, **do not add any indicator**. Mix together exactly the same amounts you used the first time.
2. Evaporate your sodium chloride solution in an evaporating basin. Remember to stop heating when about one-third is left.

Many salts are used in medicines, e.g. magnesium sulphate is used in 'milk of Magnesia', sodium chloride is used in 'saline drips' in hospitals.

Q2 (a) Do you think the salt that you have made is fit for using in medicines?
(b) How would you need to change your experiment if you were making salts for medicines?

Success for Schools: Science Book 3 – © Letts Educational 2004

24 Reacting metals with water

pp 66–67

How metals react with water

You are going to set up an experiment to look at how quickly different metals react with water. Some metals react immediately. You will need to leave your experiment set up until next lesson to see how water affects the others.

1. Half-fill five test tubes with water. Stand them in a rack.
2. Add a few drops of Universal Indicator to each.
3. Add a small amount of each of these **four metals** to separate test tubes.

   calcium (your teacher will give you this) **magnesium   iron   copper**

Q1 What did you see when you added calcium to water? What does this tell you is being made?

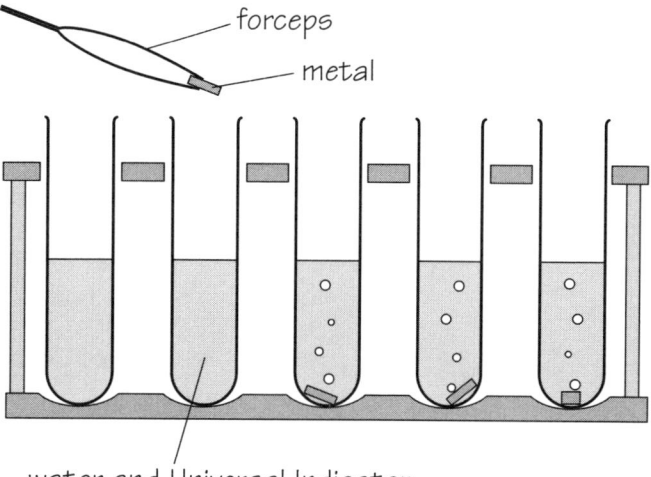

forceps

metal

4. Use the fifth test tube to repeat the experiment with calcium. This time, use a bung and a lighted splint to test the gas given off.

Q2 What does this test tell you is being made?

Q3 Write down a word equation for the reaction.

water and Universal Indicator

Thinking about Group 2

1. Watch what happens to the magnesium during the lesson. Put forward some ideas to explain what you see.

Luke did this experiment. This is what he wrote in his book:

Group 2 is the same as Group 1. The metals all make hydrogen and they get more reactive lower down the group.

Q4 Do you think Luke is right? Does he have enough evidence to say this? What further experiments do you think he should do?

Does iron make hydrogen when it rusts?

Your teacher will show you how to set up this experiment. Next lesson, find out if any hydrogen has been made.

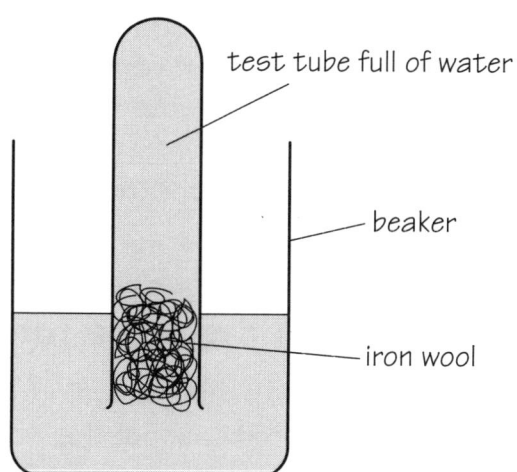

test tube full of water

beaker

iron wool

Unit 6 – Patterns of reactivity

How fast do different metals react with acids?

pp 68–69

Working out a method

You are going to investigate how fast different **metals** react with **hydrochloric acid**.

You can do this:
- *either* by measuring temperature changes,
- *or* by counting how quickly the metal makes bubbles of hydrogen.

Ann and Enjay were talking about how they were going to compare the different metals.

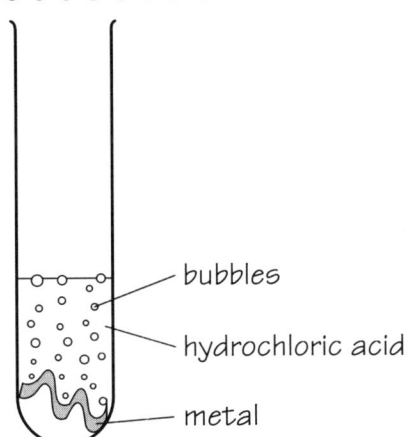

bubbles

hydrochloric acid

metal

We could count how many bubbles in five seconds.

That's not long enough. I've got another idea. We could time how long it takes to make 200 bubbles.

That's too many to count. We could do it by measuring temperature changes.

How could we do that? Anyway, whichever way we do it, we need to work out how much acid to use.

Let's measure how much acid fits in the test tube.

1. **Discuss** Ann's and Enjay's different ideas. Choose one idea and use it to plan your own experiment.
2. Do '**trial runs**' using a test tube, hydrochloric acid and magnesium to work out a method for comparing different metals.
3. Write down your **method** to show what you are going to do. Remember to design a **table** to collect your results.
4. Show your method to your teacher and carry out your experiment.
5. Think about how to show your results clearly. Would using **graphs** help?
6. Write a short report to show what you find out.

Is the pattern the same for other acids?

1. Carry out your experiment again for sulphuric acid.
2. What can you predict about the way the metals would react with other acids, e.g. nitric acid?

Success for Schools: Science Book 3 – © Letts Educational 2004

Unit 6 – Patterns of reactivity

Looking at displacement

You are going to add different metals to solutions of different salts and look to see whether you think a reaction has happened.

1. Make a large copy of this table.

	Copper	Magnesium	Zinc	Iron
copper sulphate				
magnesium sulphate				
zinc sulphate				
iron sulphate				

2. Use the reactivity series for metals on page 138 in your textbook to **predict** whether you think each pair of substances will react or not. Put a small tick ✓ in boxes where you think a reaction will happen.

3. Mix the pairs of substances together and write down your observations in your table.

4. Were your predictions right? What **evidence** do you have that reactions happened?

Q1 Write word equations for **three** of the reactions you saw happen.

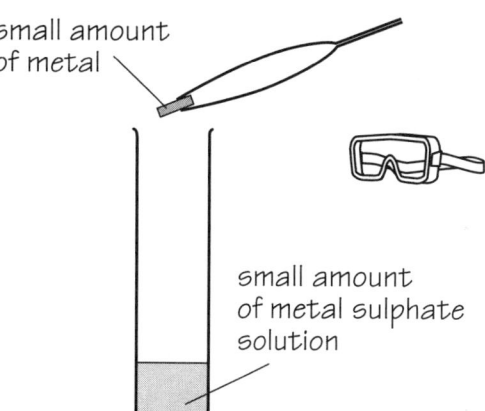

small amount of metal

small amount of metal sulphate solution

Displacement in action

1. Pour a shallow depth of copper sulphate solution into a petri dish.

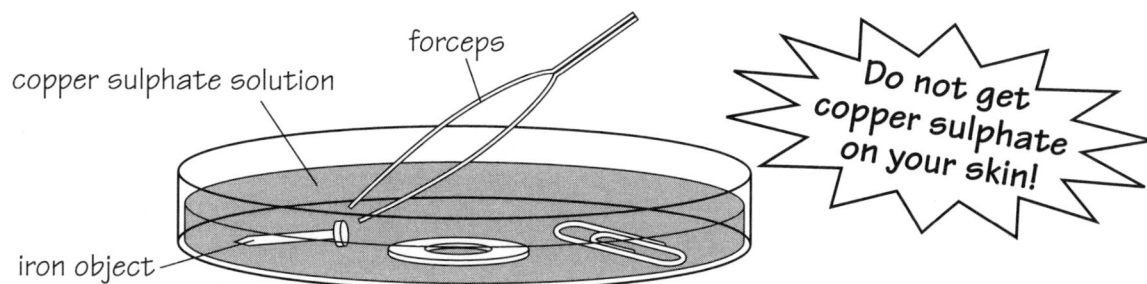

copper sulphate solution

forceps

iron object

Do not get copper sulphate on your skin!

2. Use forceps to put some iron objects into the dish. DO NOT LET THE OBJECTS TOUCH!

3. Leave the dish to stand for ten minutes, then use forceps to put the objects into a dry petri dish. What do you see?

Q2 Explain why these changes happen.

Unit 6 – Patterns of reactivity

27 Extracting metals

pp 72–73

How much metal do we make every year?

The five metals in the table are the ones we use in the biggest quantities.

Metal	UK annual production (thousand tonnes)	World annual production (million tonnes)
aluminium	248	19.5
copper	57 (recycled)	14
iron	13 000	560
lead	430	6
zinc	120	7.1

Q1 Make bar charts to show how much of each metal is made each year:

(a) in the UK,

(b) in the world.

Q2 Compare the two charts. What differences can you see?

Q3 Why do you think iron had to be left out of your charts?

LEAVE IRON OUT OF YOUR BAR CHARTS!

Extracting metals using carbon

It is cheaper to extract metals by heating them with **carbon** (in coke) than by using electricity. This table shows the **temperature needed** to extract different metals from their oxides by heating them with carbon.

Metal oxide	Temperature needed (°C)
zinc oxide	900
copper oxide	100
lead oxide	400
iron oxide	700
aluminium oxide	1600

Q4 Arrange the metal oxides in order of the reactivity of the metals. What do you notice?

Q5 Why do you think aluminium is extracted using electricity rather than by heating with carbon?

Q6 Which metal do you think is more expensive to extract, lead or zinc? Explain your reasoning.

Q7 Tin oxide reacts with carbon at 500 °C. What does this tell you about the reactivity of tin?

Q8 Choose **one** of the metals to research in more detail. Find out how it is extracted and about its uses in the UK.

28 Comparing soils

Water content

You are going to compare the water content of samples of soil that have been collected from around your school. Different groups will test different soils.

1. **Weigh** a metal tray.

2. Fill it with about **100 g of soil** and record its accurate weight.

	Fresh soil	Dried soil
Weight of soil and tray (g)		
Weight of tray (g)		
Weight of soil (g)		

3. Until next lesson, leave it in a warm place so that it dries out.

4. **Reweigh** your soil.

5. Work out the **weight of water** it contained.
   Then work out the percentage of water like this:

   $$\text{Percentage of water in soil} = \frac{\text{weight lost from soil (g)}}{\text{weight of fresh soil (g)}} \%$$

6. Mark the percentages of water on a map to show where the soil came from. Suggest **explanations** for the differences you see.

Soil pH

1. Test the school soil samples and some samples of compost to find out the pH.

2. Use a glass rod to put a drop of water onto some pH paper.

3. Design a table to show your results.

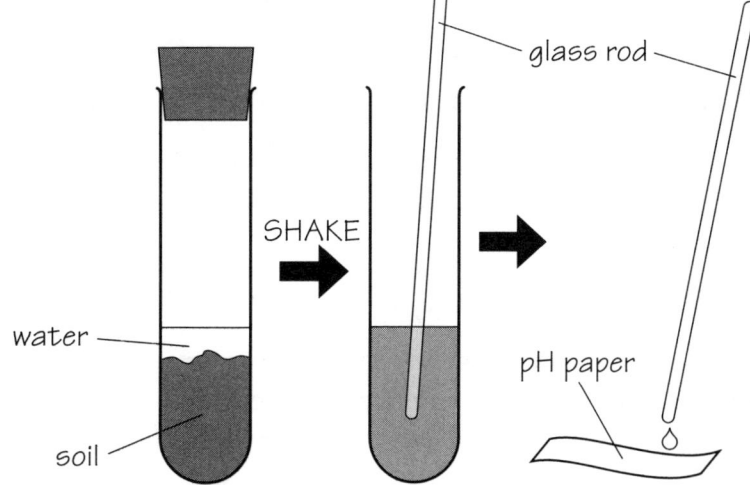

Q1 Why is pH paper easier to use than Universal Indicator solution?

Q2 Look at Figure 4 on page 74 of your textbook. Which crops would grow in soil around your school?

29 Acid rain and limestone

How fast does acid attack limestone?

You have already seen that acids react with **limestone** (calcium carbonate) and make **carbon dioxide** gas. In this experiment you will find out **how quickly** this reaction happens.

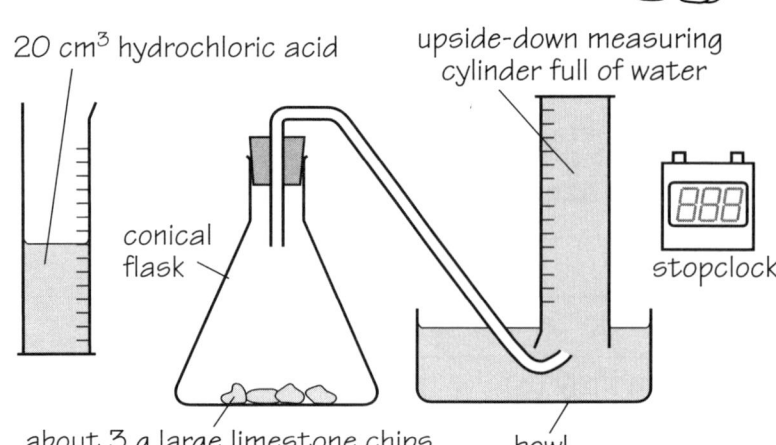

20 cm³ hydrochloric acid

upside-down measuring cylinder full of water

conical flask

stopclock

about 3 g large limestone chips

bowl

1. Set up this apparatus. Do not add your acid yet!

2. Copy this table.

Time (minutes)	Volume of carbon dioxide (cm³)		
	Limestone chips	Limestone lumps	Limestone powder
0			
0.5			

3. Add your acid to the flask, put the bung in quickly and start the stopclock.

4. Make a note of how much gas is made every 30 s (0.5 min) in the first column of your table.

5. Stop when your measuring cylinder is full or the reaction has stopped.

Q1 What do you see left in your flask at the end? Why do you think the reaction finally stops?

Using different sizes of limestone lumps

1. Do the experiment two more times using:
   - about 3 g of smaller limestone lumps,
   - about 3 g of limestone powder.

2. Record your results in the table.

3. Draw a graph with axes similar to these to show all three sets of results on one page. Plot each result using a small cross and draw a 'best fit' curve.

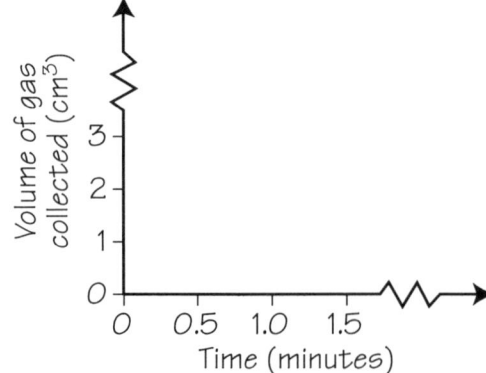

Q2 Write down what you have found out about how the different sizes of lumps affect how quickly the acid attacks the limestone.

Q3 Use what you have learnt to explain why the detail on faces of limestone statues is attacked quickly by acid rain.

30 Using limestone to neutralise acidic soil

pp 78–79 →

Making slaked lime

Farmers use limestone to neutralise acidic soil. For hundreds of years farmers made slaked lime by heating limestone in lime kilns and then adding water. They believed that slaked lime was better at neutralising acid than limestone. In this experiment you are going to find out if they were right.

1. Heat some limestone powder for about **10 minutes** using the apparatus shown in the diagram.

2. **Leave your apparatus until it has cooled down before you touch it!!**

3. Use tongs to tip your powder onto a watch glass.

4. Add about 10 drops of water, a drop at a time, and watch what happens.

You have made 'slaked lime'. Keep this for the next experiment!

5. Try adding drops of water to some limestone powder that has not been heated – watch what happens.

Q1 How does this show that heating limestone is a chemical change?

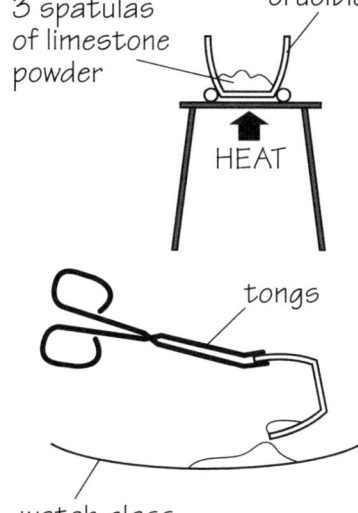

3 spatulas of limestone powder

crucible

HEAT

tongs

watch glass

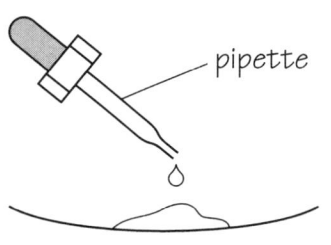

pipette

Neutralising acid soil

These three solids are all used to neutralise acid rain in soils.

limestone powder   **eggshells**   **slaked lime**

You are going to find out which one is the best.

1. Put a small amount of acid rain in three test tubes. Add a few drops of UI solution.

2. Add 3 spatulas of limestone powder to the first test tube.

3. Write down how the pH of the acid changes after each spatula is added.

4. Repeat the experiment by adding the other solids to the other two test tubes in the same way.

Q2 Which solid is best at neutralising acid rain? Explain how you can tell.

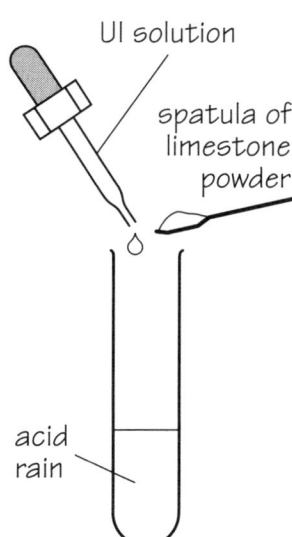

UI solution

spatula of limestone powder

acid rain

Unit 7 – Environmental chemistry

Graphs of data

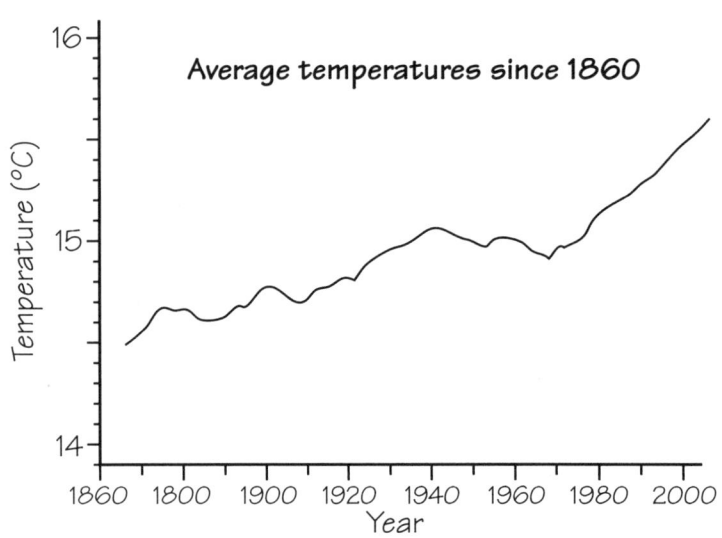

Average temperatures since 1860

Year	Concentration of CO_2 (ppm)
1850	286
1870	290
1900	295
1920	296
1940	305
1950	312
1960	318
1970	325
1980	336
1990	350
2000	366

Carbon dioxide in the air since 1850

Q1 On graph paper, draw a graph to show how the concentration of carbon dioxide in the air has changed since 1850. Your teacher will show you what axes to use.

More information about temperature changes

750 million years ago the Earth's climate was 6 °C warmer and much wetter.

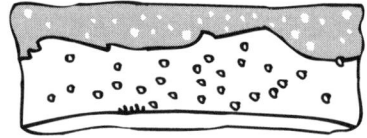

20 thousand years ago there was an ice age.

10 thousand years ago, what is now the Sahara Desert was warm and very wet.

The debate

Rose, Jojo and Diz are students. They are having a discussion about global warming.

This data proves that burning fossil fuels causes global warming. The 20th century was the warmest for 1000 years.

Rose

It doesn't prove anything – the Earth has kept warming up and cooling down for millions of years. You'd need more data to convince me.

Jojo

Well, whether we can prove it or not, we still need to stop the amount of carbon dioxide in the air from going up any more.

Diz

Task: Work as a group to research information to support the viewpoint of **one** of the three students. Use information from this sheet and your textbook to make a **short presentation** to explain your views.

pp 82–83 →

Testing fuels

People who go camping use stoves for heating water and food. You are going to look at different fuels and evaluate which one you think is best for using in camping stoves. Read the checklist 'Some features to think about when choosing a fuel' on page 83 of your textbook to give you ideas about what to look for.

1. Your teacher will show you how to safely set up and use this apparatus.

2. You are going to compare the **temperature change** in the water when the different fuels burn. You also need to look for other reasons why the fuel is either ideal or not ideal for camping.

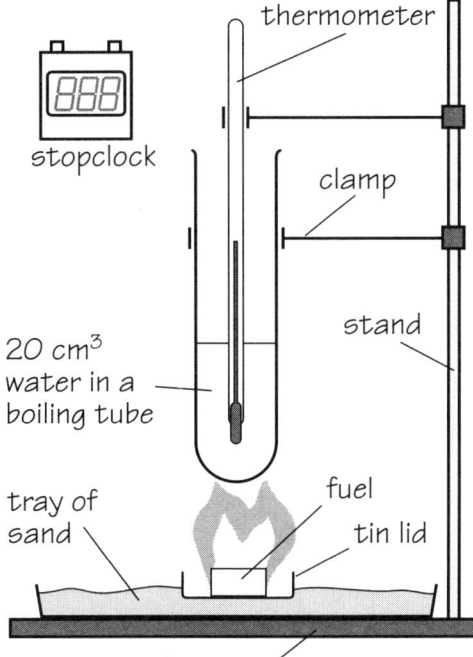

thermometer

stopclock

clamp

stand

20 cm³ water in a boiling tube

tray of sand

fuel

tin lid

heatproof mats

Remember:
- Clamp the thermometer above the bottom of the boiling tube.
- Do not touch hot apparatus.
- Put out the flame using a heatproof mat.

■ How will you make it a **fair test**?

■ **Design a table** to record your observations for different fuels.

3. Carry out your experiment.

Which is the best camping fuel?

Q1 Which fuels do you think are **unsuitable** for camping stoves? For each one, give a reason why they would not be a good choice.

Q2 Choose **one fuel** that you think could be used for camping stoves.

(a) Design a **camping stove** that could be used for heating water using your fuel. Think about how you will stop the wind blowing out the flame.

(b) Design an **advert** for your fuel. Say clearly why it is a good fuel for camping stoves.

Unit 8 – Using chemistry

33 Energy from chemical reactions

Temperature changes

You are going to carry out some reactions and measure the temperature changes that happen.

1. Repeat your experiment using these solutions. Record your observations in a copy of the table.

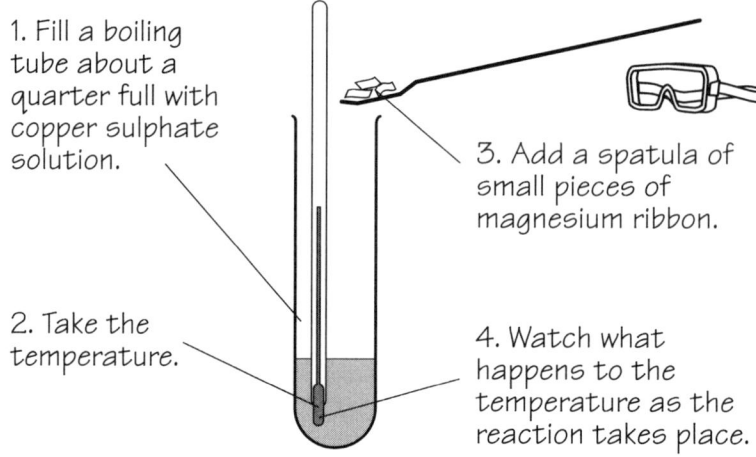

1. Fill a boiling tube about a quarter full with copper sulphate solution.

2. Take the temperature.

3. Add a spatula of small pieces of magnesium ribbon.

4. Watch what happens to the temperature as the reaction takes place.

Metal	Solution	Temperature at start (°C)	Highest temperature (°C)	Temperature change (°C)
magnesium	copper sulphate			
copper	magnesium sulphate			
iron	copper sulphate			
zinc	copper sulphate			

2. Look at the reactivity series on page 138 of your textbook to help you.

Q1 **(a)** Look at your results. Which reaction gave the biggest temperature change? Which gave the smallest?

(b) Copy and complete this sentence:
The further apart the metals in the reactivity series, the _____ the temperature change during the reaction.

(c) Why was there no change when you added copper to magnesium sulphate?

Electrical energy

1. Carry out these experiments.

2. Work out how many different pairs of metals you can make from:

iron   copper   zinc   magnesium

3. Repeat the experiments using all the metals.

4. Design a table to record your results.

Q2 How do your findings follow the pattern of your last experiment?

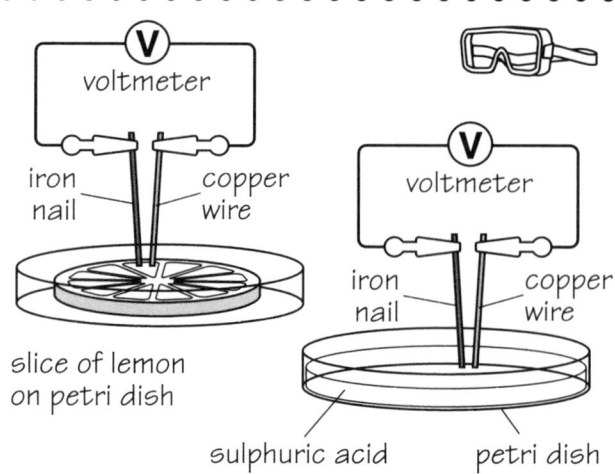

voltmeter

iron nail   copper wire

slice of lemon on petri dish

voltmeter

iron nail   copper wire

sulphuric acid   petri dish

88

34 How do soaps and detergents work?

pp 86–87

Using soap and detergent to make a lather

Some areas of the country have **hard water**. Small amounts of rock are dissolved in hard water – if you live in a hard water area you might see a lot of 'lime scale' in your kettle or around your taps. **Soft water** does not contain any dissolved rock.

You are going to carry out an experiment to compare what happens when you shake soap or detergent with hard and soft water.

> **Soap** is made from animal fats.
> **Detergent** is made using crude oil.

1. Add a few **soap flakes** to the hard water and shake until they dissolve.

2. Keep adding soap flakes, one at a time, until you can see a lather (layer of bubbles) that stays on top of the water.

3. Do the same experiment, this time using soft water.

4. Repeat the two experiments again, this time adding drops of **detergent** (using a dropper) instead of soap flakes.

5. Design a table and record your results.

Q1 **(a)** How do soap and detergent act differently in hard water?

   (b) Which do you think is 'best' to use in shampoos? Explain why.

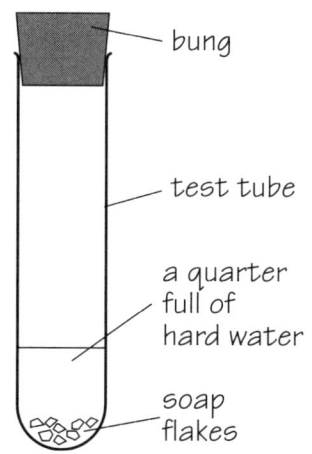

bung

test tube

a quarter full of hard water

soap flakes

Washing the oil away

You are going to use different soaps and detergents to mix oil with water. Time how long it takes for the oil layer to appear again on the surface of the water.

1. Add a few drops of oil.

2. Time how long it takes before you see the oil layer.

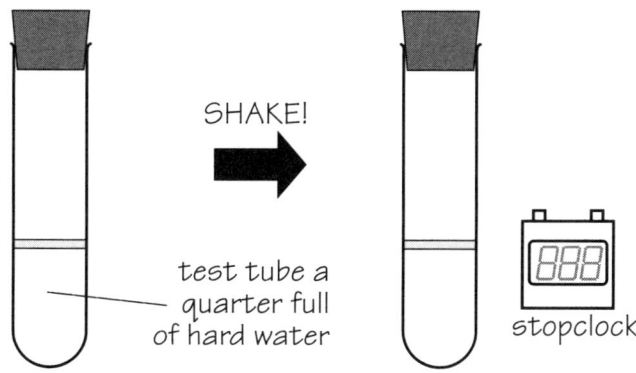

SHAKE!

test tube a quarter full of hard water

stopclock

3. Repeat the experiment, this time adding five soap flakes.

Q2 What difference does adding the soap flakes make?

4. Repeat the experiment several times, testing the different detergents available.

5. Design a table to record your results.

6. Write down what you find out.

Q3 Why does this experiment show why using detergents makes washing dirt away easier?

Unit 8 – Using chemistry

Looking at mass changes

1. Make some copper sulphate solution by reacting copper oxide with sulphuric acid. Measure the mass before and after the reaction.

REACTANTS

2 spatulas of copper oxide

25 cm³ sulphuric acid

petri dish

Measure the mass at the start

PRODUCTS

petri dish

copper sulphate solution

Measure the mass at the end

Q1 Why is it important to weigh the empty petri dish with your products?

Q2 How can you tell a chemical change has happened? Explain, using ideas about atoms rearranging, what happens to the mass during the reaction.

2. Find out how the mass changes during these reactions:

 ■ a candle burns for 5 minutes,

 ■ copper is heated for 5 minutes.

Q3 How does the mass change? Use ideas about gases to explain what you see.

Q4 What do you think is formed when copper is heated? Write a word equation for the change.

Looking at data for burning magnesium

When magnesium burns it gets heavier because it reacts with oxygen to make magnesium oxide. Here is some data from an experiment.

Mass of magnesium at start (g)	Mass of magnesium oxide formed (g)	Mass of oxygen taken from the air (g)
3	5	
6	10	
9	15	
12	20	

1. Work out how much oxygen was used from the air and fill in the last column.

2. Use your data to draw a line graph with 'Mass of magnesium (g)' up the side, and 'Mass of oxygen (g)' along the bottom.

Q5 (a) How much oxygen reacts with 4.5 g magnesium?

 (a) How much magnesium oxide would be made?

Q6 Predict how much oxygen reacts with 24 g magnesium, and explain how you got your answer.

When the Sun was forming, particles of gas (mainly hydrogen) collapsed together, like books falling from a shelf. As the particles fell together, they got faster and faster. The gas heated up.

Q1 Use ideas of energy transformation to explain why this happened.

Q2 Using the particle model for gases, explain how a hot gas differs from a cooler gas.

The Sun is a star. It is very massive and very hot – and these facts are related.

In the nineteenth century, scientists like Lord Kelvin and Helmholtz thought this collapsing of the Sun's mass under gravity could explain why the Sun shines. This early theory was proved wrong. It turns out that this collapsing process *is* important, but as the particles get hotter, something remarkable and unexpected happens – nuclear fusion. In this process, when nuclei of atoms fuse, high-energy radiation is emitted. It bounces around inside the star, and some of it eventually emerges as visible light radiation – sunshine.

Imagine a star that is forming but is more massive than the Sun.

Q3 What can we say about the gravity force causing the initial collapse of its gases?

Suppose the radiation released from deep inside the star produces a force acting to expand the star, and that this force balances the gravity force making the star collapse.

Q4 For a star to be stable and stay the same size, would you expect massive stars to be hotter or cooler than less massive stars?

During his honeymoon, James Joule spent time measuring the water temperature at the top and the bottom of a waterfall. He expected the water to be hotter at the bottom than at the top.

Q5 Can you explain why Joule expected this? What is the link with the collapse of the gas in a star?

Unit 9 – Energy and electricity

Here is a table of the names we give to some types of energy, and some characteristics of each type.

Name of energy type	Characteristics
Kinetic energy	Moving objects possess this.
Gravitational potential energy	An Earth–object system possesses this. As we pull the object away from the Earth, the Earth and the object store more gravitational potential energy.
Thermal energy	This is the random jostling of all particles in an object at some temperature. By cooling the object, we slow down the jostling. This process happens naturally when hot objects are placed in cooler surroundings.
Spring potential energy	When we stretch a spring we transfer energy to it and say that the energy we transferred is now stored as spring potential energy.
Electrical potential energy	Capacitors store this. A capacitor is a useful energy store for the flashgun used in a camera. The bigger the voltage across the capacitor, the greater the energy stored. Batteries also store electrical potential energy and are used to transfer this energy to charged particles.
Radiation energy	Heat and light from the Sun arrive as radiation energy carried on special waves. All waves transfer energy.
Nuclear energy	Deep inside an atom is a tiny nucleus. We can think of a nucleus as a tightly squashed spring, and when certain nuclei join together, or very large nuclei break into fragments, the particles formed have very large amounts of kinetic energy, which we refer to as nuclear energy.

Identify the energy types and describe the energy transfers in the following examples.

Q1 A book is pushed and released to slide along a table.

Q2 A ball is kicked high straight up into the air.

Q3 With the outlet obstructed, a bicycle pump is pumped vigorously until it becomes very hot.

Q4 A rollercoaster rushes down into a loop.

Q5 Your calculator charges up from its solar panel.

It is important that we think about energy types and energy transfers. If we do this, then we will be keeping track of energy, and that helps us understand how energy exists and is transferred everywhere in the universe.

38 Some wrong ideas about circuits and electricity

pp 94–95

Read the wrong idea about each topic, think about the work you have done on circuits, and then write in the correct idea.

Topic	WRONG idea	CORRECT idea
BATTERY	1. Batteries are a source of charge. Batteries are dead when they run out of charge. 2. Batteries are the only devices which can drive current in a circuit.	
CHARGE	3. Charge comes out of batteries and is used up in bulbs. It gets converted to some type of energy when the bulb lights.	
CURRENT: CHARGE TRAVELLING ROUND A CIRCUIT	4. Charge comes out one side of the battery. When it reaches a bulb or resistor on its journey round the circuit, charge decreases, reducing the current that flows to components further round the circuit.	
JUNCTIONS IN PARALLEL CIRCUITS	5. In a parallel circuit, charge flowing into a junction always divides equally.	

A flash camera uses a capacitor.

- A capacitor consists of two large metal plates separated by a thin layer of insulation. (A neutral piece of metal contains equal amounts of positive and negative charge.)
- When connected to a battery, mobile negative 'charges' move off one plate of the capacitor and onto the other plate. One plate is now slightly positive and the other slightly negative.
- The battery has been used to separate plus and minus charges, and the energy transferred by the battery in this process is now stored in the capacitor.
- One plate now carries more plus charges, and the other carries more minus charges. Because plus and minus charges are separated, electrical potential energy is now stored in the capacitor.

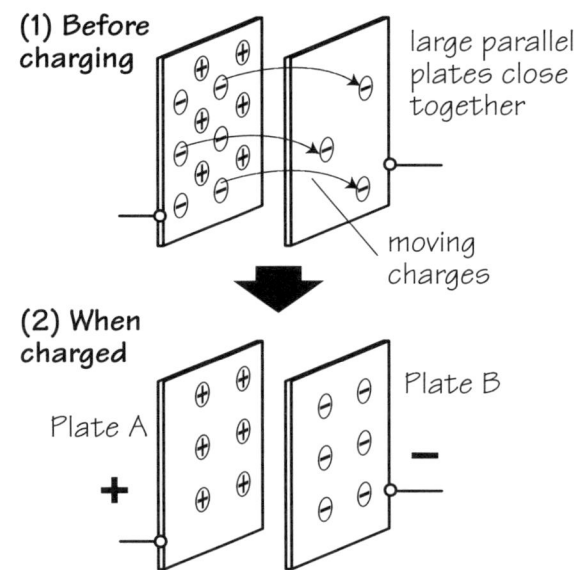

(1) Before charging

large parallel plates close together

moving charges

(2) When charged

Plate A

Plate B

+

−

Q1 To pull a negative charge off plate A and put it on to plate B, why must energy be transferred to the charges?

Q2 On a large copy of diagram (2), draw what happens if this pulling away process is repeated three more times.

This process happens very rapidly when a battery is connected to a capacitor. Chemical potential energy in the battery is transferred to increase the electrical potential energy in the capacitor:

Battery	*Battery*	*Capacitor*
chemical potential energy ⟶	electrical potential energy ⟶	electrical potential energy

We can now measure a voltage between the plates of the capacitor. This voltage tells us that the capacitor can be used to do useful tasks such as drive the flash in a camera or energise a defibrillator (a machine used to restart hearts in hospital).

1. Charge the capacitor by connecting a 6V battery across it. **Make sure you connect the positive side of the battery to the positive side of the capacitor.**

2. Allow the capacitor to discharge through a resistor. Without touching the capacitor leads, disconnect it from the battery and connect it to a resistor. Record the voltage at given intervals. This is a **slow discharge**.

Q3 Draw a graph of your results.

Warning: You MUST NEVER take a flash camera apart yourself.

3. Your teacher will show you a disposable camera circuit board. You can see the capacitor. It is used to store electrical potential energy before the flash is 'fired'. This energy is very rapidly transferred to light when a photo is taken.

4. Repeat the experiment above, but this time discharge the capacitor through an LED and see it flash.

5. Charge a capacitor using your fruit battery to make the LED flash!

Q4 Do you think that the capacitor used in this experiment stores a lot of energy?

Unit 9 – Energy and electricity

In this investigation, you are going to find out why ordinary 'incandescent' light bulbs get so hot, and why we say they are **inefficient** compared to fluorescent tubes.

The table below gives information about two types of light bulb.

Lumens are a measure of how bright a light is.

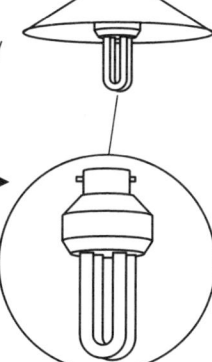

◀ **Incandescent bulb** contains a coil of fine wire that glows when electricity passes through it

Fluorescent tube ▶ contains gas that emits ultraviolet light when electricity passes through it

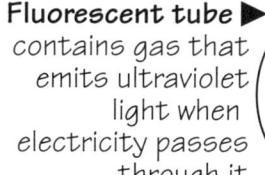

Q1 Use the data you find on the website to fill in numbers for the letters A to H.

Q2 Using your data, explain why fluorescent sources of light are much more efficient than incandescent bulbs.

While an electric current is flowing, electrons carry energy to light bulbs. The electrons transfer the energy to the metal wire in an incandescent bulb and to the gas in a fluorescent tube.

In the **incandescent bulb**, the electrons bang into the atoms of the metal wire and shake them up. The metal atoms have to be very hot before they emit light.

	Fluorescent	Incandescent
Electric power	18 watts	75 watts
Light output	1100 lumens	1150 lumens
Energy efficiency	A	B
Price per bulb	£12	30p
Rated lifetime	10 000 hours	750 hours
Cost for 10 000 hours of light:		
Number of bulbs needed	1	13
Amount of electricity needed	180 kWh	750 kWh
Cost of bulbs	C	D
Cost of electricity at 5p/kWh	E	F
Total cost of 10 000 hours	G	H

(This table of data was adapted from **http://www.public.iastate.edu/** which is a physics department site in the USA. Exact URL = **http://www.public.iastate.edu/~envr_stu_324/compacts.htm**)

A **fluorescent tube** contains mercury vapour and is coated inside with chemicals called phosphors. The electrons of the electrical current transfer energy to the mercury atoms, which do not need to get hot before they transform the energy to ultraviolet light, which we cannot see. When this light energy reaches the phosphor coating, it is transformed to visible light energy – light we can see.

Q3 Write down the sequence of energy transfers in each type of bulb. Remember: all the energy transferred must go somewhere – none of it is lost.

Q4 Can you explain why wire in the cable does not get hot, but the wire in the incandescent bulb does?

Unit 9 – Energy and electricity

pp 100–101

This torch gives 20 minutes of light after 30 seconds of shaking.

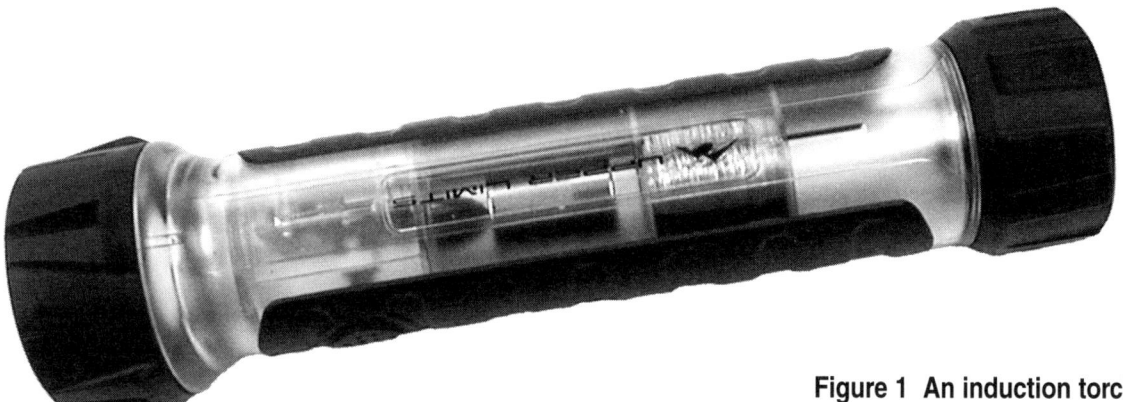

Figure 1 An induction torch

With a coil of wire and a capacitor, you are going to make a model 'shaking' dynamo to run a light-emitting diode (LED). In doing this, you will see the physics principles that govern the action of the torch.

1. Set up the circuit as shown in Figure 2.

You are going to charge the capacitor from the voltage produced as a result of moving a magnet through the coil. The diode allows more efficient charging to take place because it acts like a valve keeping the charge on the plates and allowing charging only when the magnet is moving in one direction.

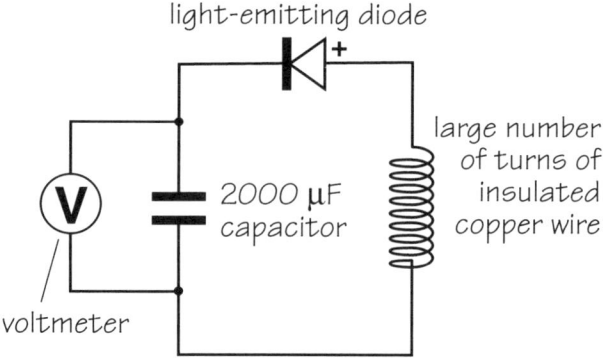

Figure 2 Dynamo and LED circuit

2. To charge the capacitor, move the magnet in and out of the coil, counting how many 'shakes' it takes to increase the voltage across the 2000 μF capacitor by 0.5 V.

3. Note how long the flash lasts, and how bright it is. This will be qualititative.

4. Draw up a table and record number of shakes, flash time and brightness.

5. Attach different capacitors, and repeat steps 2 to 4 for each one.

Q1 Does it make any difference if you change:
   (a) the speed at which you shake,
   (b) the number of turns of coils?

Remember: You have to be able to supply evidence for your answer, and it is perfectly all right if you record that changing a variable does not make any difference!

Success for Schools: Science Book 3 – © Letts Educational 2004

pp 100–101

These are some facts about generating voltage from the wind:

✱ When energy is stored in a car battery and retrieved later, 20% is wasted (dissipated) as thermal energy in the battery and its surroundings.

✱ At most, a wind turbine can extract 30% of the energy from the wind flowing through it.

✱ The electrical generators attached to the turbine are about 50% efficient for most speeds of rotation.

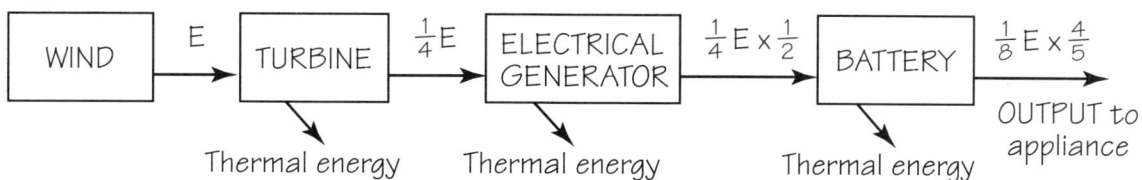

| WIND | E → | TURBINE | $\frac{1}{4}E$ → | ELECTRICAL GENERATOR | $\frac{1}{4}E \times \frac{1}{2}$ → | BATTERY | $\frac{1}{8}E \times \frac{4}{5}$ → OUTPUT to appliance |

Thermal energy   Thermal energy   Thermal energy

Figure 1 Block diagram of wind generator system

Study the block diagram. The battery is used to run appliances, but when it 'runs down' it is recharged by being attached to the generator.

Q1 Draw a diagram which traces how much of 100 J of wind energy – which is kinetic energy of the wind – ends up being available from the battery.

Q2 Describe what happens to the energy that is dissipated at each stage.

Calculating energy from wind

Read through the steps for the calculation below, and study Figure 2. Even if you cannot do all the calculation, find out the final answer – the electrical output power. It is quite low in comparison to the kinetic energy per second in the wind.

Figure 2 shows wind moving at a **speed** of 10 m/s, hitting a 2 m diameter turbine.

Q3 From the diameter of the turbine, calculate the **area** of the opening swept out by the blade as it rotates: area of a circle = πr^2.

Q4 The **volume** of air through the turbine in 1 second is: speed × area swept through by the blade. Calculate this volume if you can.

Q5 Air has a density of 1.3 kg/m³. From the volume you have calculated in Q4, work out the **mass** of air through the turbine in 1 second. Mass = density × volume.

Q6 The **kinetic energy** of this air is: ½ × mass × speed². This gives the theoretical maximum **power** of the turbine as the **number of joules per second**, also known as **watts**. Calculate in watts the power generated by the turbine.

Q7 Your answer to Q6 applies to a real turbine if it is 100% efficient. If the turbine is only 25% efficient, and the generator is only 50% efficient, how much electrical output power is produced?

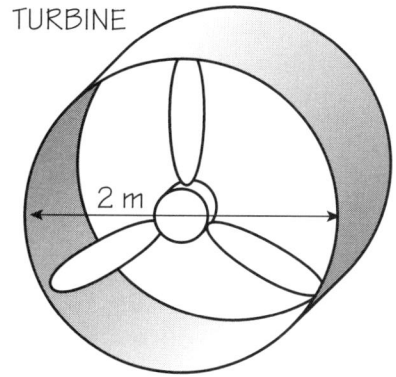

TURBINE

2 m

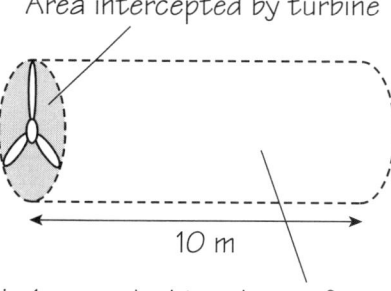

Area intercepted by turbine

10 m

In 1 second, this volume of air hits the blades at wind speed 10 m per second

Figure 2 Energy from wind

Unit 10 – Gravity and space

✳ Standing at A on the Equator at midday, the Sun's rays hit the top of your head and your shadow is a pool of darkness immediately below you. The rays will shine straight down a well at A.

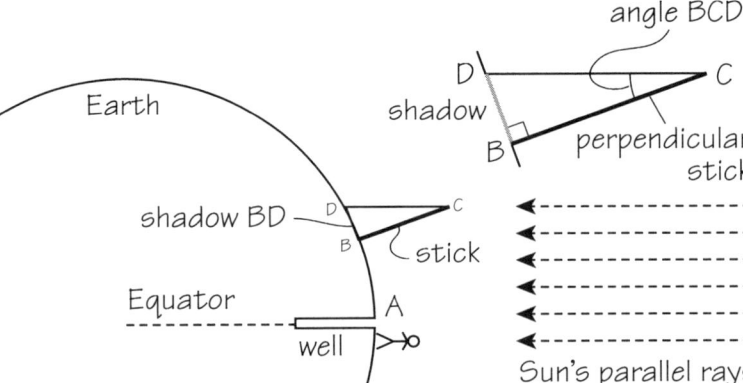

Figure 1

✳ Now imagine you go north to B and place a stick upright in the ground. Because the Earth is a sphere and its surface curved, the stick casts a shadow, BD.

✳ Knowing the height of the stick and the length of shadow, we can use trigonometry to find angle BCD shown in Figure 1.

A clever Ancient Greek named Eratosthenes did the same calculation and, knowing the distance from the Equator to the stick, he was able to find the diameter of the Earth. Now study the diagrams and follow his method.

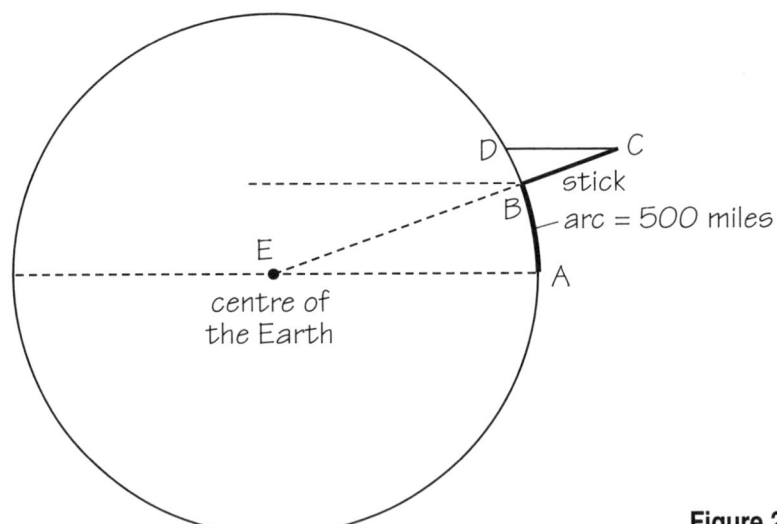

Figure 2

AB is an arc of the Earth's circumference from the Equator to the stick that Eratosthenes knew was 500 miles in length. He measured the angle BCD as 10°.

Q1 Look at Figure 2 and explain why angle BCD is the same as angle AEB, the angle at the centre of the Earth.

You can now work out the circumference of the Earth and its diameter.

Q2 If you go all the way round the Earth, how many degrees do you walk through?

Q3 Use arc length AB, the angle AEB and your answer to Q2 to find out the circumference of the Earth, and then its diameter.

By studying the Moon moving through the Earth's shadow during eclipses of the Moon, the Greeks estimated the size of the Moon in relation to Earth.

44 Gravity disappears

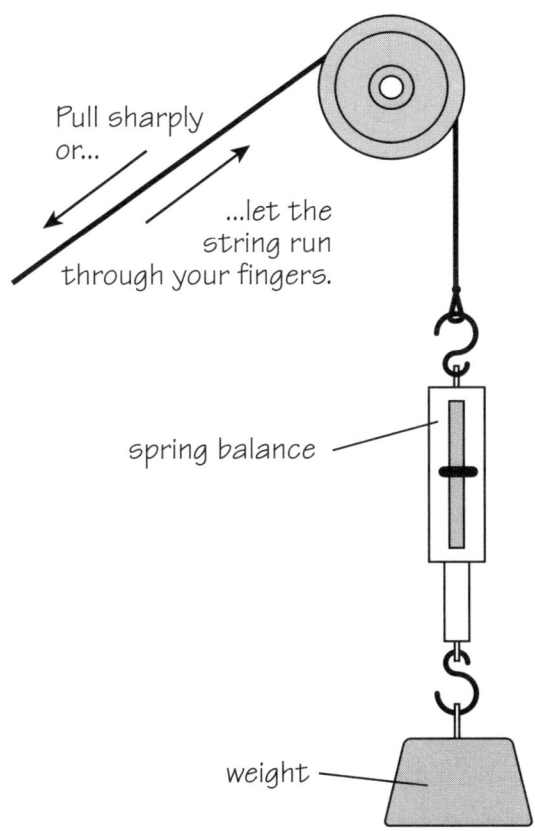

Pull sharply or...

...let the string run through your fingers.

Be careful to avoid hitting your fingers or toes with falling masses.

spring balance

weight

Figure 1

Securely attach a small mass to a spring balance. Connect the balance to a long string and pass the string over a pulley or smooth rod. You must be able to pull on the string to lift the load sharply. You must also be able to lower the load sharply by letting the string run through your fingers. Practise so that the load does not become detached from the balance.

With your partner, take it in turns to raise and lower the load. Look carefully at the spring balance reading, and write down what happens as you raise and lower the load. You will need to try several times before you can get repeatable readings from the balance.

The balance reads the weight of the mass in newtons.

Q1 Does the weight of the mass disappear, or at least reduce, in this experiment?

Q2 Einstein had some interesting ideas on this experiment. See if you can find out what he thought.

Unit 10 – Gravity and space

Fact

To get a satellite orbiting the Earth in low orbit, it must have a speed of at least 8000 metres per second.

Imagine standing on a roundabout in a park.

Q1 How does your speed change as you move away from the centre of rotation – the rotation axis – of the ride?

The Earth is rotating on its axis a bit like a roundabout. At the Equator, you are furthest from the axis of rotation. At the poles – as at the points above and below the centre of the roundabout – you are on the rotation axis.

Q2 How will your rotation speed change as you move from the North Pole to the Equator?

Q3 Where on the Earth should you launch rockets from, if you want to save on the fuel required to get a rocket to orbital speed?

Find out the latitudes of the main launch sites for rockets around the world. Visit **http://www.orbireport.com/Linx/Sites.html** and use a world map.

Q4 Does this supply evidence to back up your answer to Q3?

Unit 10 – Gravity and space

46 Bat sensor

pp 108–109

A bat sensor works by using the idea of echo-location. It uses the same method that real bats use to detect insects when hunting for food.

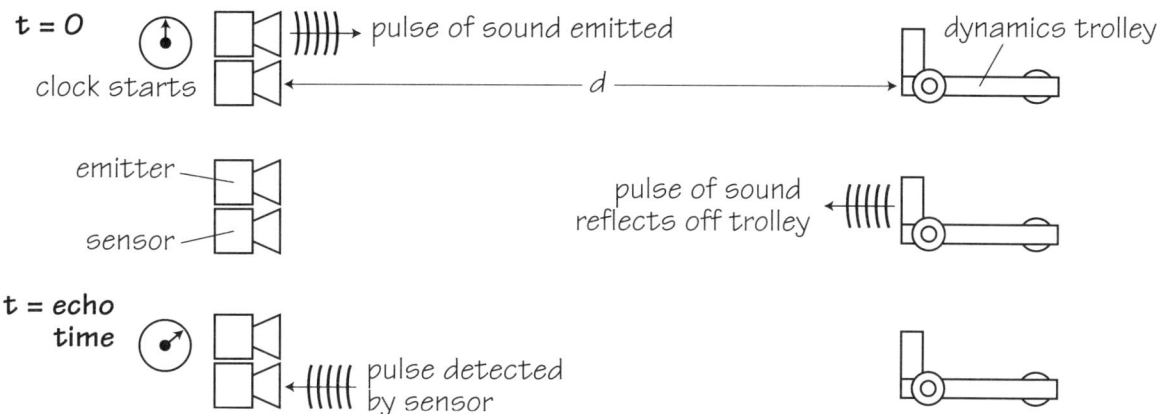

New pulse can be transmitted now.

$$\frac{\text{echo time}}{2} \times \text{speed of sound} = \text{distance } d$$

The bat sensor in use

- Ultrasonic sound waves (frequency 40 kHz) are emitted from a crystal that can also detect returning reflected sound waves of the same frequency.

- The sound is pulsed, so there are gaps between the sound waves being sent.

The bat sensor's computer times the **interval** between the transmission and detection of the sound pulses reflected by an object, and from this time interval it works out the **distance** to the reflecting object.

$$\frac{\text{echo time}}{2} \times \text{speed of sound} = \text{distance of object}$$

The computer keeps track of the object's change of position over time, and so can work out its **average speed**.

The computer can even draw position/time or speed/time graphs.

Sound travels at about 330 m/s (sound wave speed depends on air temperature), and the object being located is moving much more slowly than this.

Q1 If an object is 1 m away from the sensor, how long will it take a sound pulse to reach the object?

Q2 How long after transmission will the transmitted pulse be detected?

The speed of sound varies, so the sensor has to be calibrated to the speed of sound in the room at the time of an experiment.

To do this, the sensor is placed a **fixed distance** from a good reflecting target. This distance is inputted into the computer. Then a sound pulse is transmitted and the time taken for it to be reflected is measured. The computer uses speed = distance/time to work out the accurate speed of sound.

Q3 A reflecting target is placed 10 m away from the sensor. The time interval from transmission to receiving a signal is 0.06 s. Calculate the speed of sound to 3 significant figures.

Unit 11 – Speeding up

Look at the following tables and charts taken from around the world on the subject of car braking.

The chart in Figure 1 is based on the diagram in the Highway Code.

Typical stopping distances

20 mph [6 m] 6 m = 12 metres or 3 car lengths

30 mph [9 m] 14 m = 23 metres or 6 car lengths

40 mph [12 m] 24 m = 36 metres or 9 car lengths

50 mph [15 m] 38 m = 53 metres or 13 car lengths

60 mph [18 m] 55 m = 73 metres or 18 car lengths

70 mph [21 m] 75 m = 96 metres or 24 car lengths

Thinking distance — Braking distance

Figure 1

The table is a different way of showing the same information:

Q1 If the car-lengths table is to agree with the Highway Code data in Figure 1, what average length of car do we need?

The information in Figure 2 was taken from an Australian website. Again, it shows similar sorts of information.

A: Thinking distance in metres
B: Braking distance in metres
C: Stopping distance in metres
D: Initial speed in kilometres per hour

Q2 Create an *Excel* table that presents the data in Figure 2. Make sure that the speeds are in metres per second. Have separate columns for thinking, braking and total distance in metres.

Q3 Create a similar table for the Highway Code data. You will need to convert mph to m/s. Use 1 mile is 1600 m as the conversion factor.

Speed (mph)	Distances in car lengths for:		
	Thinking	Braking	Total stopping
20	1.5	1.5	3
30	2.5	3.5	6
40	3	6	9
50	3.5	9.5	13
60	4.5	13.5	18
70	5	19	24

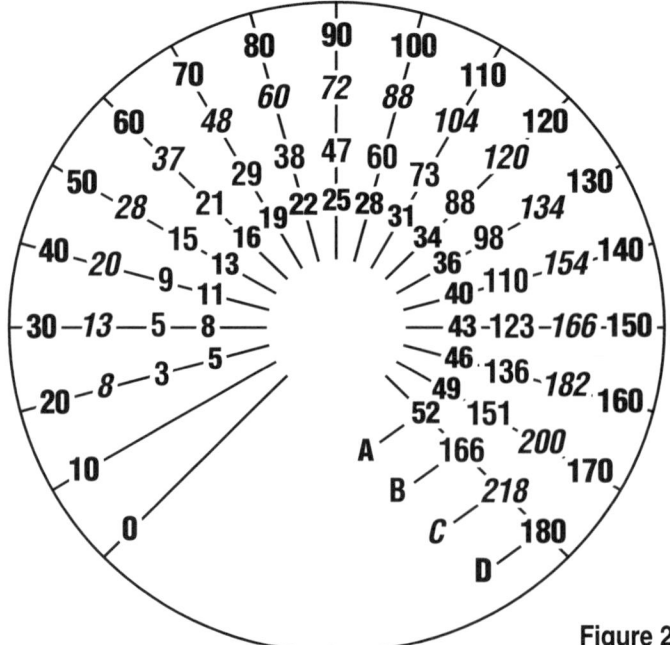

Figure 2

Big air bubble

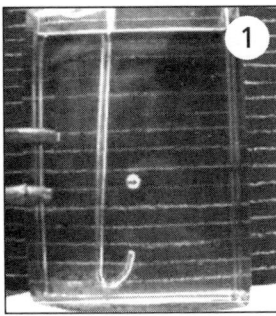
$t = 1.070$ s

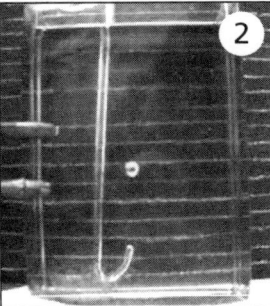
$t = 1.203$ s

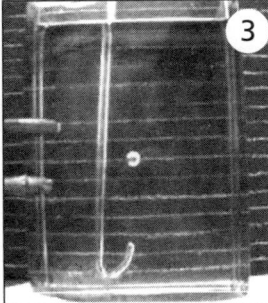
$t = 1.337$ s

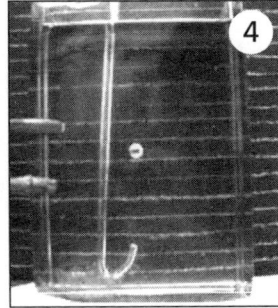
$t = 1.472$ s

Small air bubble

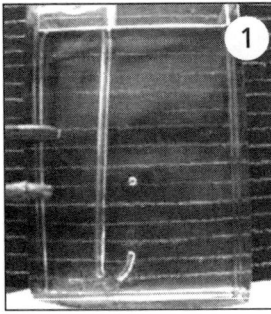
$t = 2.718$ s

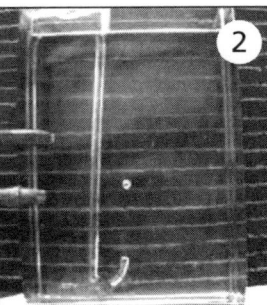
$t = 2.852$ s

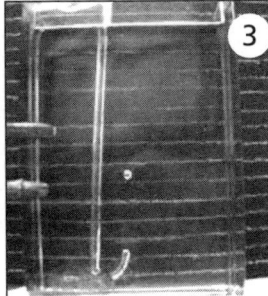
$t = 2.987$ s

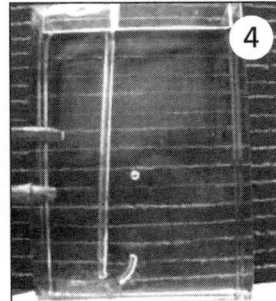
$t = 3.153$ s

Study the pictures above. They are frames taken from movies of a big air bubble and a small air bubble travelling up through glycerol.

1. For each bubble, see the times on the frames. Subtract consecutive frame times to get the time interval. Draw up a table for your data. It should show that the time interval between frames was approximately the same.

2. The table on the right shows the positions of the bubbles, measured by the scale behind the glycerol container.

3. Use your time intervals obtained from step 1 and the 'distance travelled' data in the table to calculate:

   speed = distance travelled in a time interval

Q1 Which bubble moves faster? Use your evidence and measurements to help you justify your answer.

Q2 Can you offer an explanation using forces to help you understand your answer to Q1?

Picture	Distance (cm) from bottom of bubble to line through origin	
	Big bubble	Small bubble
1	2.4	2.3
2	2.5	2.35
3	2.6	2.4
4	2.7	2.45

Unit 11 – Speeding up

The pictures show four consecutive video frames from a movie of a falling coffee filter. They were recorded at about 1/25th of a second apart.

1. Use a ruler and measure the position of the top of the filter from horizontal line X in each frame. Write the measurement on each frame clearly.

2. Use the measurements and the fact that the time interval between frames is a constant to show that the filter was travelling at a constant speed during the time of its fall in these pictures. You will need to work out:

$$speed = \frac{distance\ covered}{a\ measured\ time\ interval}$$

3. Draw a diagram showing the forces on the coffee filter, and use it to explain why the filter had reached terminal velocity.

t = 0.6833 s

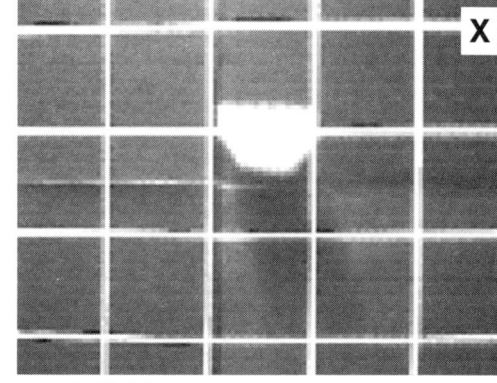

t = 0.7150 s

t = 0.7467 s

t = 0.7800 s

A typical relaxed adult inhales 28 litres of air per minute. That is on the surface, before a dive.

Let's say the volume of air in a scuba tank is 2000 litres. The air has been squeezed into a 12 litre tank – it is under high pressure. (You can store a huge volume of air in a small tank, which is useful when you have to carry a lot of air around with you.)

Q1 How long would the 2000 litres of air last on the surface?

Assume the dive is down to 30 m.

Q2 What is the local pressure on the diver at this depth? Look at page 117 of your textbook if you are not sure how to answer.

A regulating device ensures that each lungful of air from the tank enters the body at the local pressure. This means that, with increasing depth, a particular volume of inhaled gas contains an increasing number of particles. If the pressure under water is twice atmospheric pressure, then the gas will contain twice the particles, and so on in proportion.

Q3 How long will the tank last a diver at a depth of 30 m?

This experiment will allow you to study the physics of the see-saw. You will be able to work out an important law, the law of the lever, to describe the behaviour you will observe.

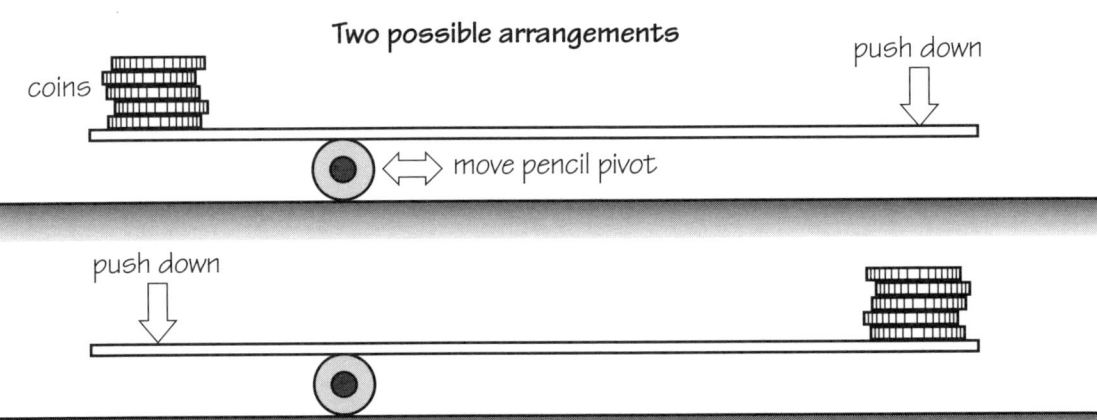

Two possible arrangements

coins

push down

move pencil pivot

push down

1. Study the diagram. Then use some small masses (nuts, washers or coins), a pencil and a 30 cm ruler, and set them up as shown.

2. Take time adjusting the position of the pivot (the pencil) and feel how much effort you need to apply to raise a fixed load. Try the experiment several times. Each time, draw a diagram, adding measurements taken from the ruler to show where the pivot was positioned in relation to the load.

3. When you have finished, clearly mark the diagram for the experiment which allowed you to lift the load most easily.

4. Write a general conclusion, saying where the load must be in relation to the pivot if it is to be lifted most easily.

Q1 A student writes that the law of the lever is 'a big load can be moved a little way by a small force providing the small force moves a big distance'. Do you agree with this statement? Use your results to discuss this student's conclusion.

5. Again for a fixed load, now try to balance the ruler by positioning a *smaller* load somewhere on the ruler. You may have to move the pivot position. Get several different balance conditions.

6. For each result, draw a diagram to record:
   • the position of the pivot
   • the position of the load
   • the position of the balancing mass
   • the mass of the load and the mass of the balancing mass

Q2 Can you see a pattern in your results?

7. Using no extra balancing masses, can you position the pivot so that a load is lifted? You may have to change the load you are using. Draw a diagram to explain why this happens.

52a Inventing the atom

pp 122–123

All things are made of atoms. The model of the atom is possibly the most important scientific idea to have been developed, over a long period of time and by many scientists. They did experiments, invented pictures, did more experiments and more thinking, and slowly developed their idea.

Dancing particles

In 1827, the botanist Robert Brown noticed that in a sample of water examined under a microscope, pollen grains 'danced' continually, no matter how long he waited for them to settle down! Brown could not explain what he saw.

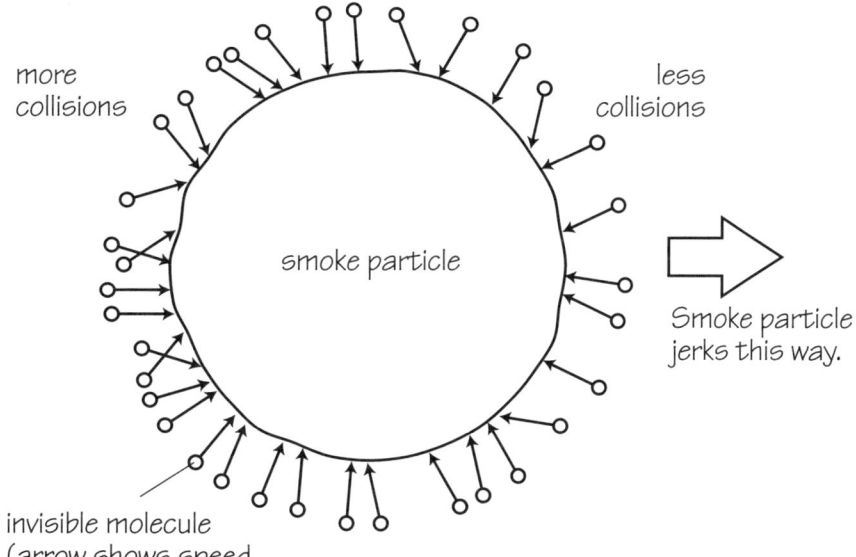

At any instant, there will be more collisions on one side than on the other.

more collisions

less collisions

smoke particle

Smoke particle jerks this way.

invisible molecule (arrow shows speed and direction)

Brownian motion

Scientists believe that the tiny particles in the air, the molecules of gas, are dancing about also. Your teacher may invite you to look through a microscope into a transparent box containing smoke. You will then see for yourself what Brown observed with the pollen grains – tiny specks of dirt, which are smoke particles, dancing around randomly.

Imagine a smoke particle surrounded by even tinier, fast moving balls that we cannot see. The balls move around randomly and collide with any smoke particle in their path, bouncing off but giving the particle a tiny kick.

Q1 Describe how this model could explain the jerky random motion of the pollen grains that Brown observed. Use the diagram above to draw some pictures of your own to help with your answer.

Success for Schools: Science Book 3 – © Letts Educational 2004

Unit 13 – Investigating scientific questions

Oil films on water

In 1900, Lord Rayleigh studied films of oil on water. He used his scientific imagination to get an estimate for the sizes of the invisible particles we used to explain Brownian motion.

Rayleigh assumed that a tiny spherical drop of oil would spread out on water, making a very thin cylinder just one molecule high.

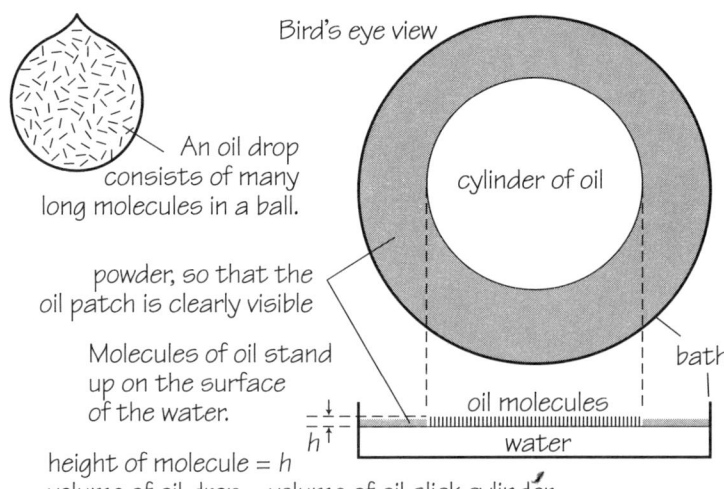

Bird's eye view

An oil drop consists of many long molecules in a ball.

powder, so that the oil patch is clearly visible

Molecules of oil stand up on the surface of the water.

cylinder of oil

bath

oil molecules

water

height of molecule = h
volume of oil drop = volume of oil slick cylinder

Rayleigh's oil drop experiment

Q2 What measurements would he need to make in order to estimate how high the oil slick cylinder is? The height of the cylinder is the length of the oil molecules.

When Rayleigh did this, for the first time people started to appreciate how small atoms must be. More evidence was needed, so others continued to explore the idea of an atom. By about 1910, a lot more was known.

Probing the atom

Scientists always have questions to ask. Rutherford investigated the 'plum pudding' model of an atom. Using the nuclei of helium atoms (called alpha particles – used today in some smoke alarms) as projectiles, he directed a beam of them at a very thin sheet of gold.

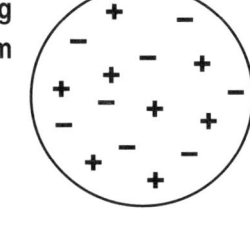

The plum pudding model of an atom

Imagine that in front of you is a large pile of light polystyrene chips. You are told that these chips conceal a heavy iron weight. You are given some tennis balls. You are not allowed to simply walk over and uncover the iron weight!

Q3 Write down what you would do to find out about the size and shape of the weight. How would your results be analysed to tell you the answers you need?

This is essentially what Rutherford did and, as a result, the atomic nucleus was discovered.

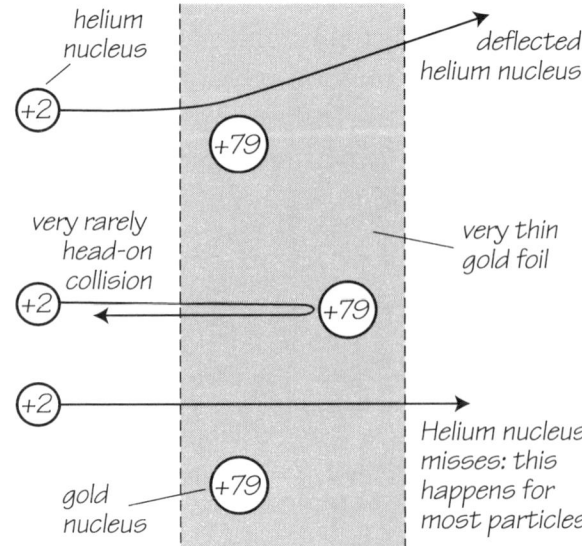

helium nucleus

deflected helium nucleus

very thin gold foil

very rarely head-on collision

Helium nucleus misses: this happens for most particles.

gold nucleus

Probing with helium nuclei